T0261197

ERP and Information Systems

Advances in Information Systems Set

coordinated by
Camille Rosenthal-Sabroux

Volume 5

ERP and
Information Systems

Integration or Disintegration

Tarek Samara

WILEY

First published 2015 in Great Britain and the United States by ISTE Ltd and John Wiley & Sons, Inc.

Apart from any fair dealing for the purposes of research or private study, or criticism or review, as permitted under the Copyright, Designs and Patents Act 1988, this publication may only be reproduced, stored or transmitted, in any form or by any means, with the prior permission in writing of the publishers, or in the case of reprographic reproduction in accordance with the terms and licenses issued by the CLA. Enquiries concerning reproduction outside these terms should be sent to the publishers at the undermentioned address:

ISTE Ltd
27-37 St George's Road
London SW19 4EU
UK

www.iste.co.uk

John Wiley & Sons, Inc.
111 River Street
Hoboken, NJ 07030
USA

www.wiley.com

© ISTE Ltd 2015
The rights of Tarek Samara to be identified as the author of this work have been asserted by him in accordance with the Copyright, Designs and Patents Act 1988.

Library of Congress Control Number: 2015948074

British Library Cataloguing-in-Publication Data
A CIP record for this book is available from the British Library
ISBN 978-1-84821-896-3

Contents

Foreword

This book written by Tarek Samara gives a relevant overview of the evolution and impact of enterprise resource planning (ERP) on information systems (IS). As he is both a professional ERP expert and a researcher, the author has a deep understanding of what is at stake nowadays in IS strategy. This book might be considered to address a paradox that has rarely been highlighted in the literature. First, it provides the readers with rich insights into the history of ERP and, going back to MRP, explains how the integration process was made possible by enterprise applications. Second, it shows how this evolution of ERP can sometimes eventually lead in itself to IS disintegration. The author does not only explore the paradox, but he also pinpoints the main factors affecting the relationships between the evolution of ERP systems and the integration or disintegration of the IS.

Thus, the author gives us a useful framework. The seven factors identified by the author are the influence of economic crisis and competitiveness on the level of IS investment, the arbitrage made by companies considering the dependency on the ERP vendor, the success or failure of the ERP project management, the interoperability of the ERP with other applications running in the IS, the choice made between two evolution strategies of existing systems (urbanization or total overhaul), the complexity level of ERP and the evolution strategy of ERP vendors such as the expansion scope of ERP perimeter. The author shows how all these factors are crucial and critical for IS management.

The outline of the book is the following. After an introduction, the first chapter describes the research terms. The second chapter deals with ERP trends. The third chapter explains the research question and methodology.

The fourth chapter explores the literature review. The fifth chapter analyzes the relationships between these research factors. In the sixth chapter, the validity of the research question is verified due to three case studies. Chapters 7 and 8 are devoted, respectively, to a discussion (relationships between research factors and the evolution of ERP systems and IS) and research interests and limitations. Finally, a conclusion is given.

The contribution of the book is threefold. First, it offers a unique typology, which gathers all the different possible ERP evolution scenarios, and highlights their impacts on IS integration or disintegration. In this way, this book is an opportunity to take stock of the different available strategies to prevent the IS disintegration.

Second, the book takes into account the main challenges faced by chief information officers (CIOs) and gives us relevant clues to foster rational selection (and purchase) of an ERP package, and improves the success of its implementation. It is definitely a recent topic because of the growing pressure of ERP vendors on their clients, and of the general context of economic crisis that tends to kill a lot of innovative information technology (IT) projects.

Finally, the book's key quality is to show that the future of ERP system evolution will not be a matter for vendors only. The book refers to the work of Freeman and raises the question of the stakeholders: firms, vendors, consultants, consultancy firms, etc. It is only by involving and taking into account all the stakeholders in the IS governance that solutions can be found. The author posits that stakeholders' participation is a key point to engage enterprises in a positive IS evolution, and advocates such kinds of corporate policy.

For all these reasons, this book could be not only useful for researchers, teachers and students but also for practitioners and IT professional experts. Its content can provide fruitful insights to anyone who wants to know more about ERP issues and how to address them.

Philippe EYNAUD
August 2015

Introduction

The evolution of enterprise resource planning (ERP) packages and the principal types or degrees of information systems (ISs) integration is to be discussed in this introduction. The factors affecting the relationships between the evolution of ERP packages and the integration or the disintegration of the ISs are also discussed.

After the first expansion, between 1980 and 2000, from "material requirements planning (MRP)" and "manufacturing resource planning (MRP II)" toward "enterprise resource planning (ERP)" considering the modules like production planning, purchasing, manufacturing, sales, distribution, accounting and human resources [ESC 99], a second evolution seems to be in progress. In order to meet the new requirements of users, it is important to take into account the framework of the ERP, new modules like "customer relationship management (CRM)", e-business, "supply chain management (SCM)", "product lifecycle management (PLM)", "business intelligence (BI)", etc. For the purpose of our research, the package which is the result of the first expansion is termed "ERP 1st Generation (1st G)" and the package that is the result of the second evolution is called "ERP 2nd Generation (2nd G)."

Various authors have written about the degree and the maturity of "information system (IS)" integration. Depending on the architecture's composition, many degrees or rates of IS integration are present today. Our study draws attention to two principal types or degrees of IS integration: a "total integration of IS (TIIS)" and a "hybrid integration of IS (HIIS)". Many studies have been conducted on the evolution of IS. This kind of research often analyzes paths of integration from a "disintegrated information system

(DIS)" to an "integrated information system (IIS)". These paths could be not only from a DIS to a HIIS or to a TIIS, but also from a HIIS to a TIIS. However, according to our study, a possible way back or a regression from integration toward disintegration (from a TIIS to a HIIS or to a DIS) has never been highlighted. Our study will discuss whether this type of regression is possible due to the evolution of ERP systems.

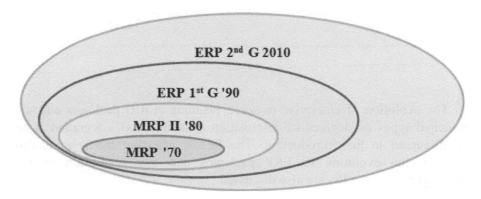

Figure I.1. *Evolution of ERP system*

As an ERP system is an indicator privileging IS integration, its selection and then its implementation by a company (which could be a success or a failure) could also be taken into account as factors that improve (or not) this integration. This study of factors as "critical success factors (CSFs)" and "critical failure factors (CFFs)" permits us to determine the evolution's trajectory of IS (toward integration or not) and also to analyze the contribution of ERPs in the IS integration. Reasonably, CSF could promote integration while CFF could prevent this integration and could even observe the IS in a state of disintegration.

This book analyzes some of the factors affecting the relationships between the evolution of ERP systems and the integration or the disintegration of the IS. More briefly, this analysis aims to study whether assigned values given to these factors could guide the evolution of ERP systems in a way that promotes IS integration; and if the assigned values opposite to the same factors could guide the evolution of ERP systems in a way that provokes IS disintegration instead.

In spite of the fact that the evolution of ERP systems is developed by vendors, this crucial mission should not be delegated solely to these vendors any more. In the future, all stakeholders (vendors, integrators, consultancy firms, clients, etc.) should be involved in the evolution of ERP systems. The experiences and the useful suggestions of integrators and of consultancy firms, as well as important feedback from clients, should also be considered. Accordingly, this research does not limit the analysis of the evolution of ERP systems to factors that are related only to vendors. The studied factors are:

– *"Economic crisis and competitiveness (ECCO)"*;

– *"Total dependency on the ERP vendor (TDEV)"*;

– *"Project management ERP (PMER)"*;

– *"Interoperability of the ERP (INTE)"*;

– *"Evolution strategy of existing systems (ESES)"*;

– *"Complexity of ERP (COER)"*;

– *"Evolution strategy of ERP vendors (ESEV)"*.

The principle behind the selection of the seven research factors is as follows:

– *"Economic crisis and competitiveness (ECCO)"* should be taken into account because of the knowledge that, during a period of economic crisis, firms hesitate to make important and expensive investments. This hesitation could impact the IS integration. "Implementation of ERP systems in many organizations is characterized by troubled multimillion dollar software deals that produce spectacular failures and large spending nightmares" [WAI 09]. Many times in ERP projects, costs exceed budgets [FIS 11, PAN 11, NAU 07]. However, companies can be motivated if a "return on investment (ROI)" calculation shows that buying an ERP system can improve their competitiveness [SHA 00, BAR 02, KAM 08, FED 09]. Therefore, the economic crisis and competitors should be studied together, as this combined factor could be involved in the determination of the IS integration rate. Moreover, competitiveness requires that companies complete the perimeter of their ISs by adding new subsystems: CRM, e-business, SCM, PLM, etc. The successful expansion of the IS's perimeter depends on the firm's evolution strategy of its existing systems;

– *"Total dependency on the ERP vendor (TDEV)"* could impact the IS integration. Firms should make an arbitrage to decide whether they prefer a dependency on an ERP vendor or not [LAM 01, NAU 07]. The IS integration rate could be different depending on this arbitrage. Total dependency means that ERP vendors should be able, within the framework of an evolution strategy, to develop and to commercialize a complete ERP (including old and new modules);

– *"Project management ERP (PMER)"* occupies an important role in the IS integration. Its success or failure leads to different rates of IS integration. "Three quarters of ERP projects are considered failures and many ERP projects end catastrophically" [RAS 05]. The success or failure of a project management is generally related to the complexity of ERP;

– *"Interoperability of the ERP (INTE)"*, which is a measure of how the ERP is interfaced or integrated with other subsystemswithin the framework of the IS, also plays a crucial role [MAR 01, BID 04b]. Interoperability could help to determine the integration rate in IS;

– *"Evolution strategy of existing systems (ESES)"* chosen by the firms is an important factor. When a company implements an ERP system within the framework of its IS evolution, there are mainly two strategies: urbanization or total overhaul. The choice of a given strategy, which depends beforehand on the state of the existing systems [RET 07, MAR 00a, LON 01], could also affect the integration rate in IS;

– *"Complexity of ERP (COER)"* could likewise be involved in the determination of the IS integration rate. ERP systems are extremely complex and difficult to implement, and many implementing companies have encountered unexpected failures [YAJ 05];

– *"Evolution strategy of ERP vendors (ESEV)"*, which defines the enlargement of the perimeter (scope) of the ERP, is also to be taken into account as an indicator of the IS integration rate. The larger the expansion of ERP perimeter, the higher the IS integration rate.

After this introduction, we will define the research terms in the first chapter. We will present the ERP: contribution and trends in the second chapter. The research question and methodology will be explained in the third chapter. The literature review (research factors affecting the relationships between the evolution of ERP systems and IS integration or disintegration) will be discussed in the fourth chapter, followed by the fifth chapter that analyzes the relationships between these research factors. The validity of the research questions is then verified in the sixth chapter by three case studies. Chapters seven and eight are devoted, respectively, to a discussion (relationships between research factors and the evolution of ERP systems and IS), research interests and limitations. Finally, a conclusion is given.

1

Definition of Research Terms

This chapter defines the research terms. We turn our attention to the definitions of the artifacts under consideration because the study of a discipline is principally the study of the language of the discipline [POS 88]. Agreed-upon terms lead to agreed-upon meanings [DAV 05].

– an enterprise resource planning *(ERP)* system is an integrated software solution, typically offered by a vendor as a package that supports the seamless integration of all the information flowing through a company, such as financial, accounting, human resources, supply chain and customer information [DAV 98]. An ERP consists of a set of fully integrated modules that run out of a single database. It covers all functions of the company and allows users to have real-time access to data. ERP systems contribute to integration in two ways, process-wise and data-wise: "the uniqueness of the database and the adoption of workflow management systems support the integration of the information flows that connect the different parts of the firm" [BER 02]. These systems are comprehensive packaged software solutions which aim for total integration of all business processes and functions [GAR 05]. For the purpose of our research, we distinguish between two types of ERP (first or second generation):

- *ERP first generation (1st G)*: we have chosen to use "1st G" to indicate an ERP system that comprises old modules only (finance, accounting, controlling, treasury, human resources, production, material management, sales and distribution, plant maintenance, project system and quality management). Most ERP systems before 2005 can be considered to be from this first generation. According to the definition of ERP, this package must be sold by one vendor,

- *ERP second generation (2nd G)*: we use the term "2nd G" to refer to an ERP system that comprises both old modules (ERP 1st G) and new modules (customer relationship management (CRM), supplier relationship management (SRM), supply chain management (SCM), product lifecycle management (PLM), business intelligence (BI), e-business, etc.). ERP systems after 2005 can be considered to be progressing toward the second generation. According to the definition of ERP, this package must be sold by one vendor.

– A *total integration of information system (IS) (TIIS)* is indicative of complete integration (integration rate is 100%); for example, when the IS of a firm consists of only one ERP system such as SAP or Oracle [ANI 01]. This ERP system could be 1st G or 2nd G, according to the users' needs and/or the implementation date (for example, 2000 or 2013).

– A *hybrid integration of IS (HIIS)* describes architecture that is more or less integrated. For example, the IS comprises different applications and ERP systems. It is a well-known fact that some legacy systems are not replaced when companies adopt the ERP solutions [THE 01]. HIIS is a set of subsystems (including ERP systems and other applications) that are more or less integrated [SAM 04].

In addition, an IS could become an HIIS when the architecture comprises many "Best of Breed (BoB)" applications. Some organizations have developed their own customized suites of enterprise applications, an approach known as a BoB information technology (IT) strategy [LIG 01]. Due to the fact that the packages of BoB applications come from different vendors, this strategy can be associated with extensive compatibility and integration issues [MAC 08].

A BoB IT strategy could also lead to an HIIS that is composed of many ERP systems. "If a customer prefers combining several ERPs by a Best of Breed approach instead of an ERP, that is fine. I simply say good luck. Such architecture could work at a given time T, but what will happen when the software in question undergoes updates? You should know that companies must make sooner or later these updates because no vendors ensure maintenance of the T minus 2 versions of its software. And every update is likely to jeopardize the integration work that holds this assembly. In short, if a company wants to spend 80% of the workforce of the IT maintenance, Best of Breed is probably a good way... But I also believe that management may be more sensitive to the functional argument of the approach that we offer with our E-Business Suite" [ANI 01].

– A *disintegrated information system (DIS)* is not at all integrated or weakly integrated. It comprises disparate legacy systems including applications and ERP systems. These applications are often not developed in a coordinated way but have evolved as a result of the latest technological innovation [THE 00]. For the purpose of our research, a DIS could consist of some applications and many ERP systems that are not at all integrated or weakly integrated in an uncoordinated way.

– An *integration rate for an information system* could be measured, according to our definition, by the presence of an integration indicator such as an ERP system and interfaces (enterprise application integration (EAI), enterprise service bus (ESB), extraction, transformation, loading (ETL), extensible markup language (XML), etc.) in the IS. Changing user needs continuously affect the IS integration rate. The integration rate is favorable (integration) when there is an increase in the ability of all subsystems in a given information system (IS) to exchange data, whereas the integration rate is unfavorable (disintegration) when there is a decrease in the ability of all components (subsystems) of a given IS to exchange data.

Elements of comparison	DIS	HIIS	TIIS
Estimated overall vision	< 50%	Between 50 and 80%	100%
Satisfaction of users' needs	Low	Between average and high	High
Architecture coherence	Low	Between average and high	High
Number of vendors	Many	Between two and many	One
Technologies used	Different and varied	Different and varied	One technology
Number of databases	Many	Many	One
Degree of coupling intersubsystems	Missing or low	Between average and high	High
Communications intersubsystems	Asynchronous	Asynchronous and synchronous	Synchronous
Interoperability between subsystems or modules	Missing	More or less effective (not native interoperability, EAI, ESB, API, ETL, XML, etc.)	Native interoperability

Number of interfaces	Neither or maybe a little bit	Many	Native interface
Estimated integration rate	≤20%	>20 and <100%	100%
Type of interfaces	Manually: different tools (universal serial bus (USB), floppy, compact disc (CD) and mails)	Manually, semi-automatic and automatic	Automatic
Importance of the interfaces' configuration settings	There are no interfaces to be configured	Very important	Priority given to the ERP system's configuration
Processing time	Batch processing	Batch and real time	Real-time processing
Evolution strategy of IS	Missing	Often an urbanization, rarely a total overhaul	Often a total overhaul is needed, rarely an urbanization

Table 1.1. *Comparisons between different degrees of integration: DIS, HIIS and TIIS*

– An *information system's perimeter* could consist of different subsystems (ERP systems, BoB applications, applications developed in-house, etc.); many examples are given in Table 1.2. Changing user needs continuously affect the perimeter of an information system.

IS No.	The IS perimeter consists of	Integration rate (IS)
1	ERP 2nd G (only one vendor)	TIIS
2	ERP 1st G (only one vendor)	TIIS
3	Different old applications developed in-house: accounting, controlling, HR, buying, selling, production, etc.	HIIS or DIS
4	BoB (many vendors): old software (accounting, HR, material management, sales and distribution, production, etc.) and/or new software (CRM, SRM, SCM, PLM, BI, e-business, etc.) A BoB IT strategy could consist of one or many ERP systems	HIIS or DIS
5	Some or all modules of IS No. 2 + some applications of IS No. 3 and/or some BoB applications of IS No. 4	HIIS or DIS
6	Some applications of IS No. 3 + some BoB applications of IS No. 4	HIIS or DIS
7	IS No. 3 + new ERP modules: CRM, SRM, SCM, PLM, BI, e-business, etc.	HIIS or DIS

8	IS No. 4 (old software) + new ERP modules: CRM, SRM, SCM, PLM, BI, e-business, etc.	HIIS or DIS
9	Some or all modules of IS No. 2 + some applications of IS No. 3 and/or some BoB applications of IS No. 4 + some new ERP modules: CRM, SCM, BI, etc.	HIIS or DIS
10	Others (e.g. many different ERP systems)	HIIS or DIS

Table 1.2. *Examples of the various perimeters of information systems in firms*

For IS numbers 3–10, the architecture could be an HIIS when all subsystems are integrated, whereas it could be a DIS when all subsystems are not integrated.

– *An integration of information systems* is, principally, the increase of the integration rate; that is an increase in the ability of all subsystems in a given IS to exchange data. For the purpose of our research, integration means a progression from DIS to HIIS or to TIIS and also from HIIS to TIIS. For example, a migration toward a total integration is a transformation from IS numbers 3, 4, 5, 6, 7, 8, 9 or 10 to IS number 1 (Table 1.2).

– *A disintegration of information systems* is, principally, the decrease of the integration rate; that is a decrease in the ability of all components (subsystems) of a given IS to exchange data. Disintegration indicates a regression from TIIS to HIIS or DIS and from HIIS to DIS. In other words, disintegration is the converse of an integration. For example, changing from IS numbers 1 or 2 to numbers 3, 4, 5, 6, 7, 8, 9 or 10 (Table 1.2).

– *Scenarios of disintegration (some examples)*: we suggest three main reasons that could maintain or provoke the IS disintegration:

1) Firms desire to improve the integration of their IS but fail to select an ERP system (before implementation) because of some factors. This scenario leads to keeping the existing system that is already disintegrated. It may even increase its disintegration due to the evolution of users' needs.

2) Firms fail to implement their ERP system because of some factors. This situation cannot help the IS integration.

3) After implementing an ERP 1st G, firms fail to continue to upgrade this package toward an ERP 2nd G. According to this scenario, firms prefer to combine this ERP 1st G with others' ERP packages or applications. Therefore, a kind of integration regression could affect the IS during its evolution from the ERP 1st G to the new target.

– Examples of IS integration (firm X) and IS disintegration (firm Y): we suppose that an ERP 1st G, which was able to achieve an IS integration rate of about 100%, satisfied most users' needs in 1998. After the appearance of new users' needs (CRM, SCM, PLM and BI), the ERP 1st G became unable to satisfy all users because its level of integration decreased in the IS. From 100% in 1998, the level of integration became 70% before 2014. In fact, a given integration rate could decrease due to the appearance of new needs of users.

The old integration rate of 100% no longer applies, but it could be again recuperated depending on how the new needs are taken into account. Generally, according to the approach chosen by firms to evolve their IS, it is possible to determine if there will be integration or disintegration. A migration toward an ERP 2nd G, which allows a return to the initial rate of 100%, is a kind of IS integration. However, a migration from an ERP 1st G toward an IS numbers 5 or 9 (Table 1.2) signifies a kind of disintegration. In this case, the integration rate of 100% achieved initially by one ERP 1st G, which was alone in the IS, is decreased.

Example of IS integration (firm X: Figure 1.1 and Table 1.3):

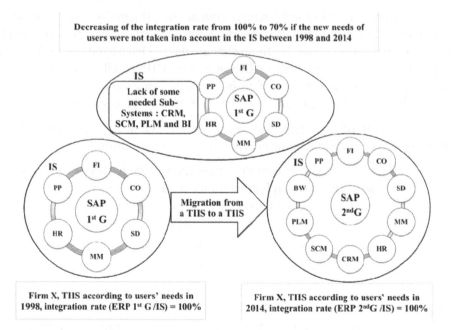

Figure 1.1. *Example firm X: migration from TIIS toward TIIS (maintaining the initial integration rate despite the evolution of users' needs)*

	TIIS		TIIS
Date	**1998**	**2014**	
Evolution of users' needs	Modules ERP 1st G	Modules ERP 1st G + new needs (CRM, SCM, PLM and BI)	
IS Integration rate (hypothesis 1)	100% (Architecture consists only of an ERP 1st G)	Became 70% due to the appearance of new needs of users which were not taken into account in the IS between 1998 and 2014 (the architecture is still composed only of an ERP 1st G)	
IS Integration rate (hypothesis 2)	100% (Architecture consists only of an ERP 1st G)	Becomes 100% again if the new needs of users are taken into account between 1998 and 2014 (the IS consists only of an ERP 2nd G)	

Table 1.3. *Example firm X: migration from TIIS toward TIIS*

Example of IS disintegration (firm Y: Figure 1.2 and Table 1.4):

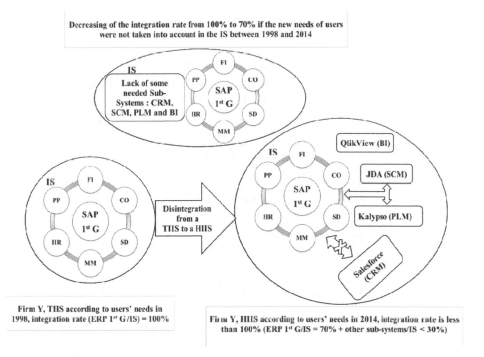

Figure 1.2. *Example firm Y: disintegration from TIIS toward HIIS*

	TIIS	HIIS
Date	**1998**	**2014**
Evolution of users' needs	Modules ERP 1st G	Modules ERP 1st G + new needs (CRM, SCM, PLM and BI)
IS Integration rate (hypothesis 1)	100% (Architecture consists only of an ERP 1st G)	Became 70% due to the appearance of new needs of users which were not taken into account in the IS between 1998 and 2014 (the architecture is still composed only of an ERP 1st G)
IS Integration rate (hypothesis 2)	100% (Architecture consists only of an ERP 1st G)	70% (by ERP 1st G) + less than 30% (by other sub-systems because CRM and BI are not integrated) if the new needs of users have been taken into account between 1998 and 2014
Evolution of IS	ERP 1st G	IS No. 5 or 9 (see Table 1.2) other subsystems
IS perimeter	ERP 1st G SAP	ERP 1st G SAP + other sub-systems (QlikView, JDA, Kalypso and Salesforce)

Table 1.4. *Example firm Y: disintegration from TIIS toward HIIS*

– Research factors: the seven variables that will be studied in order to determine the relationships between the ERP system's evolution and the IS integration or disintegration (Table 1.5).

Research factor (variable)	Acronym
Economic crisis and COmpetitiveness	ECCO
Total dependency on the ERP vendor	TDEV
Project management ERP	PMER
INTEroperability of the ERP	INTE
Evolution strategy of existing systems	ESES
COmplexity of ERP	COER
Evolution strategy of ERP vendors	ESEV

Table 1.5. *Factors affecting the relationships between the ERP system's evolution and the IS integration or disintegration*

ERP: Contribution and Trends

This chapter illustrates the role and trends for enterprise resource planning (ERP) implementation within the framework of the information systems. It also shows the main trends related to the evolution of ERPs toward a new generation (2nd G).

2.1. ERP as an indicator of integration for information systems

This indicator aims to illustrate the contribution of ERP systems to the integration of information systems. Many studies that have been conducted on the evolution of information system (IS) principally show its transformation toward integration. Scientists consider system integration as one of the most problematic areas of ERP implementation [THE 01, RAT 12]. Firms should use ERP as an integrative mechanism to create a new style of management [HAM 99]. An ERP system is an IS that manages, through integration, all aspects of a business [ESC 99].

Many companies started to replace their legacy system with ERP packages in order to solve integration problems during the 1990s [HYV 03]. The integration of applications is one of the main reasons for the ERP system adoption [SPA 04]. Any ERP system pushes a company toward full process integration and solves the fragmentation of information [PAR 05]. ERP systems can be viewed as tools for control and integration [HAN 06]. ERP systems aim to integrate business processes into a synchronized suite of procedures, applications and metrics that exceeds firms' boundaries [WIE 07].

Firms implement ERP systems to integrate the business processes of a company [DIX 11]. Bidan *et al.* emphasize the lack of integration that results from the absence of ERP systems within information systems [BID 12]: "The 'Silos Architecture' category is strongly characterized by the lack of ERP systems, and therefore has a large number of autonomous applications which do not utilize a common logical database. The architecture looks like a set of heterogeneous applications with few interfaces. The logic of the Silos Architecture is not that of integration in the pure sense but simply of limited or controlled interoperability". An implemented ERP system is almost always becoming the core system for information collection and processing, so it needs to integrate data from each organizational level and functional area: manufacturing, distribution, sales, etc. [RAT 12].

Consequently, we can consider an ERP system to be an indicator of IS integration. For the purpose of our research, the selection of an ERP system and then the success or the failure of its implementation by a company can be used as an indicator to measure the integration rate for its information system.

2.2. Trends for ERP implementation within the framework of the information system

The prospect of replacing "home grown" legacy systems with the integrated business solution offered by ERP systems, such as SAP/R3, PeopleSoft and Oracle, has proven to be irresistible [CAL 98]. For instance, many firms prefer to use ERP systems when they set out to replace the legacy system [HOL 99]. The outgoing legacy systems are usually associated with the title of a "dying system" [ALV 00]. However, organizations typically do not "abandon all their existing applications when adopting ERP solutions" [SCH 00]. ERP systems have not solved the integration problems as many companies do not abandon their legacy systems and they integrate their functionality from disparate applications. It has also been argued that ERP packages have in fact failed to achieve (a total) application integration and 38% of companies which adopt these ERP solutions do not replace their legacy systems [THE 01].

If you look closely at the level of ERP presence in firms, it is clear that almost all large companies are equipped with at least one, if not several, ERP systems. More than half of all small- and medium-sized enterprises (SMEs) have an ERP system. Some large groups have launched several ERP systems. A survey shows that, on average, large groups have 2.7 ERP systems each and some have many more [ELA 07]. A large group that had 22 different ERP systems has initiated a project to remove 18 of them [DES 04]. "One ERP, to cover all needs, has proved largely illusory" [DES 04]. Today, the functionality of universal and modern ERP systems includes almost all standardized business processes. Therefore, in some cases, the activity area of a company (e.g. public institutions) or specific legal considerations (e.g. the case of salary calculations) are unique. Consequently, to evaluate ERP software suitability, we have to consider its integration possibilities with software already in use [RAT 12].

Mabert *et al.* surveyed 479 US manufacturing firms [MAB 00] and found that more than 60% of companies have installed or plan to install a packaged ERP system. According to Gartner [BIS 09], the ERP software market is still growing; overall, the enterprise software market in Europe, the Middle East and Africa was expected to reach 70 billion euros by 2013, with a 5-year compound annual growth rate (CAGR) of 5.0%. During the same period, it was estimated that the worldwide market would reach 214 billion euros, with a CAGR of 7.1%. The need to integrate all the business processes in one computer system and align this system with the business goals in today's highly competitive world has only become more important.

Ventana Research 2010 (White Paper) reported that one-third of companies with more than 1,000 employees use an ERP application supplied by a single vendor, while two-thirds use software from two or more vendors; of the latter, one-third have software from four or more vendors [VEN 10]. There are largely two reasons why companies have heterogeneous ERP environments. One is purely historical: automating back office functions began decades ago, and companies initially did not roll out or upgrade the systems across the entire enterprise. Moreover, some parts of the organization may have been built through acquisitions. If the acquired entity was relatively large, it often made sense to leave the existing systems in place.

These heterogeneous ERP environments could also be related to a "Best of Breed (BoB)" information technology (IT) strategy. The various advantages of BoB implementation include less disruption to an organization, less required process reengineering and the allowance for greater flexibility [MAC 08]. Like ERP systems, "Enterprise Application

Integration (EAI)" also encourages the use of BoB applications from multiple vendors [BID 12]. This means that an IS can comprise many ERP systems, which could be themselves a kind of BoB.

Bidan *et al.* identified two categories of positioning for ERP systems within the framework of the IS [BID 12]:

1) the "Partially Standardized Architecture";

2) the "Mixed Architecture".

The "Partially Standardized Architecture" category is characterized by the limited coverage of the ERP (in terms of the number of modules installed). One hundred percent of the firms of this class have a unique ERP, 90% for at least one module for its support activities and 77% for its core activities. However, 77% of the firms in this category have from one to three modules deployed and one to three silos architecture. Eighty-three percent of reporting firms with partially standardized architecture do not have an EAI platform and have no common database. The integration in this category can be described as having some limited ERP implementation (single vendor only), also having software bridges in addition to the ERP system and achieving integration via the ERP and any additional software bridges.

The "Mixed Architecture" category is the most advanced with regard to IS architectural and systems integration because this organization type mixes EAI and ERP systems [SHA 05]. This category is characterized by having common database models, widespread use of an ERP system with integration standards arising from the greater adoption of the ERP modules and combining ERP and EAI technologies in various ways [KHO 06]. Within this category, Bidan *et al.* found that 29% of the firms do have common databases. Most (83%) have one ERP system, and a few (17%) have more than one. Firms in this category have at least a core activity module (92%), and a support activity module (88%). Many of these firms have from four to eight ERP modules in place (62%), with more than one-third (35%) having eight or more ERP modules. In transitioning to ERP, most firms appear to have abandoned autonomous applications in favor of the ERP system's core operations (81%) and support activities (79%). They often have an EAI platform (65%) as well. Nearly one-third of these firms are among the largest firms of our total sample. This category represents the closest match to Markus' broad category of the hybrid firm [MAR 00a].

These trends for ERP implementation within the framework of the information system illustrate that one ERP could rarely occupy the whole IS alone. Often, the architecture consists of many ERP systems and/or other subsystems. For this reason, in this book, we principally study two types of integrated information systems: total integration of IS (TIIS) and hybrid integration of IS (HIIS).

2.3. Trends for ERP evolution toward a new generation (2nd G)

Bowersox called for more effort to be exerted toward the integration of supply chain systems using ERP systems [BOW 98]. ERP is the information backbone of supply chain management [ALM 00]. The emphasis on supply chain management and the advancement of information technology created a need for enterprise-wide integration [HIS 04]. Firms seek to use ERP systems to establish integration with other supply chain stakeholders [MAC 08].

The top management of the organization can choose to change the IS either by the addition or deletion of new processes to take advantage of and exploit dynamic environmental conditions that can be improved by interconnecting clients and suppliers [RAS 10]. In order to facilitate supply chain management (SCM) operations for business planning and decision making, an ERP system must be extensible in terms of support for a range of external constituents in the supply chain [CHU 11].

In this regard, the Ford Motor Company was able to connect customers' warranty information with suppliers to help improve future products. The ERP market leaders constantly upgrade their production quality characteristics with new versions. According to a consultancy study by AMR Research [SWA 04], 55% of upgrades have been voluntary business improvements triggered by the need for a new functionality, expansion or consolidation of systems. The systems, applications and products for data processing (SAP) grows with the enterprise, as further modules and resources can be installed and configured as needed [UFL 07].

Some articles attempt to understand the direction of the industry regarding ERP extensions. A few articles explain the enabling of technologies through further ERP extensions and integrations. Some reports research on how to expand the existing functionalities of the ERP system. Vendors are continuously increasing the capabilities of their ERP system by adding additional functionality such as business intelligence, supply chain and customer relationship management (CRM), etc. [STE 01]. "After having insisted that their software package treats all the essential business functions, ERP vendors offer for sale new essential modules" [DES 04]. As most ERP vendors have now developed a broader definition of enterprise integration, these articles may well provide a good picture of the trends which essentially deal with the issues of extending ERP systems toward e-business, supply chain management, customer relationship management, supplier relationship management, business intelligence, manufacturing execution systems, etc. [MOO 07].

As a result, we can assume that ERP 1st G systems have become incomplete by today's standards (lack of some modules relative to users' current needs) and therefore are not able to satisfy all needs. We can notice the appearance, since the year 2000, of new users' needs which should be taken into account as new modules (CRM, SCM, product lifecycle management (PLM), E-business, information system for decision making, (ISDM), etc.) within the framework of the ERP evolve from 1st toward 2nd G.

3

The Research Question and Methodology

This chapter presents the research question and methodology. Researchers have often built their analyses on the fact that enterprise resource planning (ERP) is a package contributing to the information system (IS) integration. As a result, research has not made sufficient effort to study the possible involvement of ERP systems in IS disintegration, although such a possibility could exist. Whatever the reason for the disintegration, the lack of investigation in this field is significant and it should be studied. A possible disintegration or regression from a total integration of IS (TIIS) to a hybrid integration of IS (HIIS) or to a disintegrated information system (DIS) will be taken into consideration in our book. This matter could be important because practitioners and end users who manage an ERP project to improve the architecture's integration could sometimes be surprised once the project ends and the ERP is deployed. Instead of a desired integration, a kind of IS disintegration can occur. For example, within an IS, an evolution from an ERP 1st G toward a new architecture could lead to a regression of the integration rate which existed before this evolution.

This chapter aims to understand and explain the main reasons why these unwanted scenarios could happen. Knowing these reasons allows all stakeholders to avoid these scenarios, which could lead to IS disintegration instead of integration. This research attempts to explore and identify eventual relationships between the evolution of ERP systems and IS integration or disintegration. The aim of our research is to know if the relationships between the ERP systems and the IS are guided by certain factors and, as a result, this study intends to understand, more in-depth, the factors affecting these relationships.

As an ERP is an indicator of IS integration, the selection of a suitable package and the success of its implementation could improve the integration of the existing system. By contrast, the failure of an ERP system's implementation cannot promote IS integration but could rather maintain the existing system in a state of disintegration. Therefore, the literature review related to ERP selection criteria and to main reasons for the success or failure of ERP implementation is our point of departure.

The study and analysis of this literature review enabled us to identify certain factors which establish and guide the relationships between the evolution of ERP systems and the IS. We have derived and deduced, from this literature review, the seven research factors (Economic crisis and competitiveness (ECCO), Total dependency on the ERP vendor (TDEV), Project management ERP (PMER), Interoperability of the ERP (INTE), Evolution strategy of existing systems (ESES), Complexity of ERP (COER) and Evolution strategy of ERP vendors (ESEV)). These relationships typically lead the IS toward integration, provided that some defined values of these factors are met. However, when these defined values are not satisfied, the desired integration could be replaced by a kind of disintegration. In other words, the values improving IS integration, which have often been studied in the literature, help to deduce logically the opposite values which will not help IS integration and could rather provoke its disintegration.

Consequently, the identified factors are variables that need to be rated or evaluated because they are able to take different values. This rating helps to evaluate the impact of the values taken by each of these seven factors on IS integration or disintegration. The purpose of our research is to know whether a given arbitration by firms and/or by ERP vendors related to these factors (choosing defined values for these variables) could guide the evolution of ERP systems and therefore impact IS integration or disintegration.

Based on the literature review and on a logical analysis, it was possible to measure each variable and to give it two different values: positive and negative. Each value allows us to measure a different impact of the ERP system's evolution on the IS and thus to study various possibilities of evolution. A positive value is attributed when this factor promotes IS integration; while a negative value is given when this same factor provokes IS disintegration instead of its integration. Globally, IS integration is obtained when the values of these factors are often positive; when these values are often negative, IS integration could be compromised.

The literature review also permitted us to determine some correlations between these variables. For example, causal correlations are used to indicate that a change in one variable could be the result in changes in other variables. Many combinations and interactions can exist between these factors and it is useful to explore them. This research tries not only to discover and understand the values of these factors, but also to analyze their interactions.

With these concerns in mind, the main research question is: *are there some factors that could explain the role of ERP system evolution in guiding the IS toward integration or disintegration?* In order to investigate the main research question, the following subquestions were derived:

– Should the competitiveness of a firm, especially within the context of economic crisis, be a criterion to be taken into account by all stakeholders within the framework of an ERP system's evolution? If so, would IS integration be favored? If not, would its disintegration be provoked?

– Should the dependency of a firm on vendors be a criterion to be taken into account by all stakeholders within the framework of an ERP system's evolution? If so, would IS integration be improved? If not, would its disintegration be initiated?

– Should a methodology for optimizing project management, based on best practices, be a criterion to be taken into account by all stakeholders within the framework of an ERP system's evolution? If so, would IS integration be improved? If not, would its disintegration be possible?

– Should improving interoperability be a criterion to be taken into account by all stakeholders within the framework of an ERP system's evolution? If so, would IS integration be improved? If not, would its disintegration be initiated?

– Should firms' evolution strategies of existing systems be a criterion to be taken into account by all stakeholders within the framework of an ERP system's evolution? If so, would IS integration be improved? If not, would its disintegration be provoked?

– Should simplifying the complexity be a criterion to be taken into account by all stakeholders within the framework of an ERP system's evolution? If so, would IS integration be improved? If not, would its disintegration be possible?

– Should the evolution strategy of ERP vendors from 1st to 2nd G be a criterion to be taken into account by all stakeholders within the framework of an ERP system's evolution? If so, would the IS integration be improved? If not, would its disintegration be initiated?

To achieve our research goal, we need to study the ERP system's evolution, as well as the IS and the factors that can explain relationships between them. The theoretical framework is deduced from reviewing the literature and searching for other online sources (newspapers, interviews, online literature, etc.). Due to the lack of literature in the field of IS disintegration, we conducted an empirical study based on practitioners' experiences via newspapers and interviews with professionals. The interviews were found mainly on the Internet, and the respondents held various relevant positions, such as ERP vendors, integrators, consulting firms, chief information officers (CIOs), consultants, project teams and end users, etc. This range of varying perspectives enabled us to collect several complementary points of views. Data triangulation was conducted to increase the reliability of our study.

The research methodology involves case studies that are used to explore the relationships between the evolution of an ERP system and IS integration or disintegration. Case study research is suitable for descriptive and exploratory research [BAX 08]. The proposed factors (variables) were verified and evaluated, and then they helped us to select case studies whose comparison could serve to identify patterns and findings [YIN 04]. The findings from case studies are provided, and the research propositions are reviewed, verified and improved.

Three case studies have been conducted: the first two case studies analyze the IS of firms; while the third case study studies the strategy of an ERP vendor. We analyzed some famous existing case studies (Hershey and FoxMeyer Drugs) retrieved from the literature. Many authors had analyzed these case studies from their point of view, while we studied them from another point of view related to the goal of our research. We believe that viewing the observations and interviews through the framework of the real-world case studies is the most valuable method to explore and understand the relationships between the evolution of an ERP system and IS integration or disintegration. We also found many interviews (web articles) with practitioners who answered questions related to the research question and the third case study (vendor Oracle). As a result, the comparison between three different case studies and the analysis of the review of the literature, followed by our interpretations and deductions, helps to reply to the research question.

We summarize the research methodology in the following stages:

– exploratory and descriptive, focused on the literature review, allowing us to have the necessary knowledge to better structure our analysis and to deduce our findings [EIS 89, EIS 07];

– inductive to develop a research field, such as IS disintegration, with little theoretical knowledge [SIG 07];

– qualitative by case studies, which allow us to validate or invalidate the analysis deduced from the review of the literature;

– interpretative because a discussion is being presented from the results of the prior research and the case studies, from which a conclusion is drawn.

We view this research as contributing to the description of the unusual relationships between ERP systems and IS. The analysis of ERP systems' evolution and IS integration or disintegration is derived from a description, exploration and interpretation of the literature rather than being derived from a statistical analysis. Why? Because we are, principally, looking to highlight some new tendencies in the progress of evolution for which considerable observation is necessary. In summary, we determined that a mainly inductive approach together with a qualitative research method is the most appropriate way to fulfill the purpose of our research. Finally, this research methodology leads to the development of a typology by which we can establish some tendencies allowing researchers and practitioners to develop more knowledge in this field.

4

Literature Review: Factors Affecting the Relationships between the ERP System's Evolution and IS Integration or Disintegration

This chapter gives a description of the literature review. Given that an enterprise resource planning (ERP) is an indicator of information system (IS) integration, it is important to study some interaction factors between ERP systems and the IS. Within this perspective, the ERP system's selection criteria and then the success or failure of the ERP implementation are crucial factors to consider. The analysis of the literature helped us to discover the appropriate factors that impact the IS evolution's trajectory, thereby allowing us to reply to the research question.

Kumar *et al.* [KUM 03] analyzed a practical survey of 20 enterprises in Canada of ERP selection criteria (functionality of the ERP, better fit with company's business processes, fit with parent/allied organization systems, cross-modular integration, best business practices available in the system, system reliability, implementation project management, vendor reputation, availability of regular upgrades, compatibility with other systems, vendor's support/service infrastructure, ease in customizing the system and lower costs of ownership).

Grabski *et al.* [GRA 03] confirm that an ERP system's implementation differs from more traditional IS implementation in terms of scale, complexity, organizational impact and the costs involved. Umble *et al.* [UMB 03] mention the following criteria: price, supplier support, ease of implementation, closeness of fit to the company's business, flexibility when the company's business changes and value (total implementation cost vs. total value to the company).

Verville and Halingten [VER 03] suggest a list of selection criteria: customization; user interfaces; whether the organization's existing database management system is compatible with the proposed solution; the ability of the proposed solution to integrate into the organization's existing hardware architecture; the architecture of the proposed solution (client/server, two-tier, three-tier or other); scalability of the system; training (in-house or external to the organization; does vendor conduct the training or is outsourced?); performance; ability to assist the organization with the implementation; the association with or the availability of third party vendor/partners; vision future plans and trends regarding the direction of the technology and/or strategic positioning; financial strength; product recognition; ability to meet future needs; reputation; vision and/or strategic positioning of the vendor; longevity of the vendor; qualifications, experience and success in delivering solutions to organizations of a similar size, complexity and geographic scope; quality of the vendor's proposal; demonstrated understanding of requirements, constraints and concerns; implementation plan that properly positions the proposed solution to achieve the maximum level of business benefits; implementation services; implementation strategy; and support services.

Fisher and Kiang used the following criteria to evaluate ERP packages: service and support, training, scalability, implementation flexibility, integration, manufacturing process, core financials, purchasing and sales, human resource process, support fees and training fees [FIS 04]. Han mentions many ERP selection criteria: vendor, functionality and scalability [HAN 04].

Wei *et al.* identify six system software factors and three vendor factors. System software criteria are total costs, implementation time, functionality, user friendliness, flexibility and reliability [WEI 05]. Vendor criteria are reputation, technical capability and provision of ongoing services. Keil and Tiwana synthesize the ERP selection criteria: cost, reliability, functionality, ease of use, ease of customization, ease of implementation and vendor reputation [KEI 06]. Lall and Teyarachakulmenion synthesize four ERP selection criteria: complexity of implementation, estimated cost of implementation, functional match and vendor profile [LAL 06].

Ayağ and Özdemir [AYA 07] discuss the following criteria: system cost (license fee, vendor support, maintenance cost and infrastructure cost), vendor support (good reputation, consulting performance, research and development (R&D) capability, technical-support capability and training performance), flexibility (upgrade ability, ease of integration and easy of in-house development), functionality (module completion, function fitness and security level), reliability (stability and recovery ability), ease of use (easy of operations and easy of learning) and advanced technology (standardization, integration of legacy systems and easy to maintain). Yang *et al.* [YAN 07] mention the importance of an ERP system's acceptance by end users (hardware requirements, compatibility with old hardware, hardware upgrade capability, fitness of available modules, acceptance by middle-to-high-level managers and working load for end users).

Bueno and Salmeron [BUE 08] identify many criteria related to ERP systems: the capacity to integrate the ERP system with the current IS/information technology (IT), trust in the ERP system, modularity, adaptation of the ERP to the current system needs, software costs, consultation costs, maintenance costs, parameter complexity, employee continuing education, traditional organizational culture, complexity of the organizational structure, traditional organizational strategy and complexity of organizational processes.

In the research performed by the Aberdeen consultancy group [ABE 06, ABE 07], 1,245 and 1,680 companies, respectively, of different size, industries and geographical regions, have participated. As a result, we defined the three ERP selection factors cited most frequently. Functionality has been named as the most important criterion (in 69 and 75% of cases, respectively). In 53% of cases, the system price has been mentioned. Ease of use was the third most popular factor, cited in 42 and 51% of cases, respectively. The surveys performed in the years 2008 and 2009 by the same group have shown and confirmed the previous results.

Ratkevičius *et al.* [RAT 12] studied 12 of the most important software-related ERP selection criteria: ERP functionality, total costs of ERP implementation projects, vendor reputation, ERP reliability, ease of integration with other systems, advanced technology, scalability, upgrade ability, customization/ parameterization possibilities, ease of use, flexibility and modularity.

In summary, when a firm wants to select or buy an ERP package, there are some crucial interrogations to help guide the selection process:

– Would it be possible to pay the "Total Cost of Ownership (TCO)" and can the return on investment (ROI) be positive within the framework of an economic crisis?

– Would the firm's IS be independent or completely dependent on the ERP vendor (in other words, the ERP system is it modular or would it be possible to buy a part [i.e. certain modules] of the ERP system only)?

– Will ERP project management be a success or a failure (what are the risks)?

– Is it an interoperable ERP?

– Which strategy will be adopted by clients to integrate the ERP system within the framework of the existing system (urbanization or total overhaul)?

– Is it a complex or a simple ERP system?

– What is the evolution strategy of ERP vendors?

Beyond the ERP selection criteria, many authors have performed significant research to identify critical factors in ERP implementation. Several academics and practitioners have tried to capture the main reasons for the success or failure of ERP system implementations [EWU 97, GLA 98, LAU 99, SWA 99, PAR 00, SOH 00, SUM 00, MOT 02, MAJ 03, STA 04, WEI 04, ANE 06, KIM 06, IBR 08, LIN 08, PAR 09]. Most of these analyses and lists focus on the factors that contributed to failure rather than the factors that contributed to success. There are many factors that appear on most of the lists: top-level management support for the project, user training and education, project management, project team competence and change management, process and organizational adaptation, measurement of the benefits, resistance to change, scalability and scope, and ERP importance.

Some researchers investigated the "Critical Success Factors (CSFs)" of ERP implementation. CSFs of ERP have been demonstrated by an extensive number of publications: [DAV 98, BIN 99, SHA 99, BRO 99, CAN 99, GRI 99, HOL 99, LAU 99, KUM 00, JAR 00, PAR 00, WIL 00, ALM 01, CHE 01, EST 01, NAH 01, ROS 01, SOM 01, AKK 02, HON 02, MUS 02, VER 02, MAB 03, SPA 03, UMB 03, COL 04, RAS 05, SUN 05, ALM 06, KIN 06, PLA 06, FIN 07, KHO 07, BRA 08, BUE 08, ELS 08, NGA 08, SHA 09].

However, some researchers studied the "Critical Failure Factors (CFFs)" of ERP implementation. For example, failure factors were highlighted in the following papers: [YEO 02, SHO 05, TSA 05, MOM 10]. Kumar *et al.* [KUM 10] did a study to prioritize the issues affecting an ERP system in a medium-scale fertilizer company and the following factors were determined: training and testing, employee retention, customization and external consultant dependency. The CFFs are defined as the key aspects where "things must go wrong". This means that these critical failure factors could compromise the reliability of the IS integration, and thus a kind of disintegration in the IS architecture could be happened.

For the purpose of our research, we have classified, organized and grouped the literature within the framework of seven main factors as shown in Table 4.1. All of the articles reviewed were related to ERP selection criteria and to the main reasons for the success or failure of ERP implementation.

Themes, of the literature review, used to determine = the research's factors affecting the relationships between the ERPs' evolution and the IS integration or disintegration	Authors (literature review)
High costs, lower costs of ownership, software costs, consultation costs, maintenance costs, ROI, business implications of ERP implementations, strategic impact of ERP implementation on a firm's competitive advantage, competitive strategy, reductions in costs, reductions in customer lead times and production times, reducing total time from order to delivery, improve competitiveness, value, (total implementation cost vs. total value to the company), estimated cost of implementation, competitive advantage and profitability, organizational bankruptcy = **ECCO (Economic Crisis and Competitiveness)**	Bulkelery, 1996; Scott, 1999; Kumar and Hillegersberg, 2000, Davenport 1998; Akkermans *et al.*, 2003; Umble, Haft and Umble, 2003; Gunn, 1998, Somers and Nelson, 2001; Ayağ and Özdemir 2007; Majed, 2000 ; Markus *et al.*, 2000; Ptak, Schragenheim, 2000; Sadagopan, 1999; Bueno and Salmeron 2008; Fisher, Fisher and Kiang, 2004; HsiuJu Rebecca Yena *et al.*, 2004 ; Keil and Tiwana, 2006; Lall and Teyarachakul 2006; Rao 2000; Grabski *et al.* 2003; Umble, Haft and Umble 2003; Kumar, Maheshwari and Kumar 2003; Wei, Chien and Wang 2005; Leon 2007; Yang, Wu and Tsai 2007; Mabert, Soni and Venkatraman 2000; Bernroide, Koch 2001; Severin V. Grabski, Stewart A. Leech, Lu Bai 2001; Aberdeen's 2007 study; Hitt, Wu, & Zhou, 2002; Kalling, 2003; Kennerley and Neely, 2001; Mabert *et al.*, 2001; Poston and Grabski, 2001; Hayes *et al.*, 2001; Robinson and Wilson, 2001; Hitt *et al.*, 2002; Hunton *et al.*, 2002; Gattiker and Goodhue, 2002; Beretta, 2002; Hunton *et al.*,

	2003; Somers *et al.*, 2003; Spathis and Constantinides, 2003; Stensrud and Myrtveit, 2003; Spathis and Constantinides, 2004; Hedman and Borell, 2004; Nicolaou, 2004; Gattiker and Goodhue, 2004; Huang *et al.*, 2004a; Spathis and Ananiadis, 2005; Chand *et al.*, 2005; Tsai *et al.*, 2006; Ziaee, Fathian and Sadjadi, 2006; Wieder *et al.*, 2006; Wu and Wang, 2006; Spathis, 2006; Lall and Teyarachakul, 2006; Ayağ and Özdemi, 2007; Leon, 2007; Uflacker and Busse, 2007; Yang, Wu and Tsai 2007; Bueno and Salmeron, 2008; Aberdeen group, 2006, 2007, 2008 and 2009; Trabelsi *et al.*, 2013.
external consultant dependency, ERP modularity = **TDEV (Total Dependency on the ERP Vendor)**	Dhénin, 2001; Themistocleous *et al.*, 2001; Kumar, Maheshwari and Kumar (2002, 2003); Rowe *et al.*, 2005; Ziaee, Fathian and Sadjadi, 2006; Naugès, 2007; Uflacker and Busse, 2007; Bueno and Salmeron (2008); Vijaya Kumar *et al.*, 2010; Bidan *et al.*, 2012; Ratkevičius *et al.*, 2012.
training and testing, Customization/parameterization, employee retention, support from top management, ERP project efficiency, user knowledge, project team competency, change management = **PMER (Project Management ERP)**	Anderson and Narasumhan, 1979; Barki, *et al.* 1993; Bulkelery, 1996; Ewusi-Mensah, 1997; Davenport, 1998; Holland and Light, 1999; Jiang and Klein, 1999; Markus *et al.*, 2000; Grabski *et al.* 2003; Verville and Halingten, 2003; Wei, Chien and Wang, 2005; Stapleton and Rezak, 2004; Weightman, 2004; Anexinet, 2006; Kimberling, 2006; Nah and Delgado 2006; Ziaee, Fathian and Sadjadi, 2006; Yang, Wu and Tsai 2007; Ibrahim, *et al.*, 2008; Lindley, *et al.*, 2008; Chen, R. 2008; Vijaya Kumar *et al.*, 2010; ParijatUpadhyay, 2010.
standardization, integration possibilities with the legacy systems, capacity to integrate the ERP with the current IS/IT, integrate other specialized software products with the ERP suite, exchange data and enable sharing of information, interoperate implies that one system performs an operation for another system, ease of integration with other systems = **INTE (INTEroperability of the ERP)**	Bingi *et al.*, 1999; Everdingen, 2000; Sprott, 2000; Markus, 2001; Papazoglou and Georgakopoulos, 2003; Irani *et al.*, 2003; Sharif *et al.*, 2005; Jamison, Layman, Niska, Whitney, 2005; Bueno and Salmeron, 2008; Naugès, 2008; Chen *et al.*,2008; Maheshwari and Kumar (2002, 2003); Verville and Halingten, 2003; Konstantas *et al*, 2005; Jamison, Layman, Niska, & Whitney ??; Ayağ and Özdemi, 2007; Moon, 2007; Leon, 2007; Bidan *et al.*, 2012; Ratkevičius *et al.*, 2012; Trabelsi *et al.* 2013.
traditional organizational strategy, traditional organizational culture, complexity of the organizational	Davenport, 2000; O'Leary, 2000; Themistocleous, Irani, & Love, 2002; Bueno and Salmeron, 2008; Verville and Halingten,

structure, complexity of organizational processes, organization's existing compatible with the proposed solution, can the proposed solution integrate into the organization's existing hardware architecture?, compatibility and adaptability of ERP with old systems and with other systems, modernize the IS by erasing the legacy systems, modernize the IS without erasing the legacy systems, changes within an organization = **ESES (Evolution Strategy of Existing Systems)**	2003; Yang, Wu and Tsai 2007; Kumar, Maheshwari and Kumar 2003; Hopkins & Jenkins, 2008; Trabelsi *et al.*, 2013.
user-friendly interface and operations, ERPs are complex systems, ease of customization, ease of implementation, case of integration, ease of use (easy of operations and easy of learning), parameter complexity, vendor's complexity, simplicity of training and use, using ERP intuitively without additional specific knowledge, complexity due to the ERP complexity = **COER (COmplexity of ERP)**	Pivnicny and Carmody, 1989; Ciborra *et al.* 2000; Everdingen 2000; Schönefeld and Vering, 2000; Hanseth *et al.*, 2001; Grabski *et al.*, 2003; Verville and Halingten, 2003; Wei, Chien and Wang (2005); Kumar and Hillegersberg, 2000; Ciborra *et al.*, 2000; Hanseth *et al.* 2001; Bueno and Salmeron, 2008; Verville and Halingten, 2003 ; Lall and Teyarachakul 2006; Keil and Tiwana 2006; Ayağ and Özdemi, 2007; Uflacker and Busse, 2007; Yang, Wu and Tsai (2007); Leon, 2007; Ratkevičius *et al.*, 2012; Aberdeen group, 2006, 2007, 2008 and 2009.
module completion, scalability and scope and ERP importance, complete functionality, ERP functionality, system reliability, extension, vendor's vision (future plans and trends regarding the direction of the technology and or strategic positioning), product recognition, vision and strategic positioning of the vendor, longevity of the vendor, qualifications, experience, domain knowledge suppliers, technically upgradable, functional match and vendor profile, vendor profile (prompt availability of software upgrades and technical support), adaptability of ERP system (employed system technologies, embedded database system, system development tool and language), availability of	Goldenberg *et al.*, 1991; Pivnicny and Carmody, 1994; Chau, 1995; Hecht, 1997; Everdingen *et al.*, 2000; Rao 2000 ; Siriginidi, 2000; Schönefeld and Vering, 2000; Chen, 2001; Bernroider and Koch 2001; Stensrud, 2001; Nah, Faja, Cata, 2001; Verville and Halingten (2003); Kumar, Kumar and Maheshwari 2002, 2003; Scott and Kaindl, 2000; Zheng *et al.*, 2000; Tarn *et al.*, 2002; Willis and Willis-Brown, 2002; Choi and Kim, 2002; Sumi and Tsuruoka, 2002; Yen *et al.*, 2002; Lee *et al.*, 2003; Weston, 2003; Akkermans *et al.*, 2003; Rutner *et al.*, 2003; Newell *et al.*, 2003; Symeonidis *et al.*, 2003; Kovács and Paganelli, 2003; Ash and Burn, 2003; Ng and Ip, 2003; Verville and Halingten, 2003; Gulledge *et al.*, 2004a; 2004b; Frank, 2004; Bendoly and Kaefer, 2004; Davenport and Brooks, 2004; Koh and

regular upgrades, R&D capability of vendor, importance of choosing a suitable ERP vendor (reputation, technical capabilities and provision of ongoing services), functional match and vendor profile, uses latest technology, upgrade ability of the ERP vendor, functional match (capability of the ERP to meet the business requirements of the firm), adaptability of ERP system (employed system technologies, embedded database system, system development tool and language) = **ESEV (Evolution Strategy of ERP Vendors)**	Saad, 2004; Barthorpe *et al.*, 2004; Ndede-Amadi, 2004; Cardoso *et al.*, 2004; Han, 2004; Swanton 2004; Chou *et al.*, 2005; Burn and Ash, 2005; Moon and Phatak, 2005; Moller, 2005; Bendoly and Schoenherr, 2005; Lea *et al.*, 2005; Jaiswal and Kaushik, 2005; Kelle and Akbulut, 2005; Biehl, 2005; Burca *et al.*, 2005; Sammon and Adam, 2005; Wei, Chien and Wang (2005); Keil and Tiwana 2006; Lall and Teyarachakul 2006; Sharma *et al.*, 2006; Although Liao, Li and Lu 2007; Johansson, 2007; Uflacker and Busse, 2007; Yang, Wu and Tsai 2007; Bueno and Salmeron 2008; ParijatUpadhyay, 2010; Aberdeen group, 2006, 2007, 2008 and 2009.

Table 4.1. *An alignment of the literature with the main factors affecting the relationships between the ERP's evolution and IS integration or disintegration*

As stated previously, values were assigned to each research factor. This evaluation helps to determine the impact that each of these seven factors (variables) has on IS integration or disintegration.

We can notice from the literature review two main possibilities:

– the first is the ERP system's selection and then the success of its implementation. This scenario could logically improve the IS integration;

– the second possibility is the failure of the ERP implementation, or, before implementation is even possible, the rejection of the ERP system (e.g. the ERP system's selection is postponed). This scenario could promote IS disintegration instead of integration.

In other words, we deemed those variables that can improve the IS integration to be positive values (first possibility). Based on this logic, we attributed negative values when the ERP system's evolution could lead to IS disintegration instead of its integration (second possibility).

The seven identified factors or variables (ECCO, TDEV, PMER, INTE, ESES, COER and ESEV) will be studied below in more detail.

4.1. Economic crisis and COmpetitiveness (ECCO)

Legacy systems have been described as having a "consequentially negative impact on competitiveness" [BRO 95] while being "non-maintainable and inflexible" [O'CA 99]. In order to improve this competitiveness, authors have advised to implement an ERP. Akkermans *et al.* supported the strategic impact of ERP implementation on a firm's competitive advantage [AKK 03]. In the past few years, ERP has become a "must have" system for almost every firm to improve competitiveness [HSI 04]. The ERP can be considered an integration tool that is able to help the competitiveness of the company [PER 04]. Competitive priorities clearly affect the practices of ERP implementation in many aspects. The ERP system is implemented to support these competitive priorities. The authors confirm that ERP implementation should be aligned with competitive strategy.

However, Davenport suggested that firms should restrain from ERP investment until further study of its business implications is fully understood [DAV 98]. The cost of ERP is significant and failure can result in the demise of the organization, as in the case of the FoxMeyer Drugs bankruptcy [SCO 99].

Total cost of ERP project (TCO) is a selection criterion that is mentioned quite often by Mabert *et al.*, Bernroide and Koch, Umble *et al.*, Fisher *et al.*, Wei *et al.*, Keil and Tiwana, Lall and Teyarachakul, Yang *et al.*, Bueno and Salmeron, Ratkevicius and others [MAB 00, BER 01, UMB 03, FIS 04, WEI 05, KEI 06, LAL 06, YAN 07, BUE 08, RAT 12]. Most researchers include as part of the TCO: an upgraded technical infrastructure, software licenses, ERP implementation, support, maintenance, consultant fee and user training. Summarizing different definitions, ERP costs include all ERP implementation and usage costs (both direct and indirect) during the total lifetime of the system. Direct expenses involve hardware, software and implementation costs. Indirect, or hidden, expenses are related to productivity drop during the ERP implementation period when activity outage or stoppage occurs.

Firms experiencing unprecedented economic crisis tend to delay major ERP projects considered to be too expensive. Pending a more stable environment, they favor, in principle, secondary short-term projects. However, in a state of economic crisis, companies operate in a difficult environment: saturated markets, increased competitiveness, customers more demanding and less loyal, etc. In such an environment, the competitiveness of enterprises depends on the reliability of their IS integration internally as well as their mode of communication with partners (customers, suppliers, etc.).

According to Ayağ and Özdemi [AYA 07], ERP selection criteria are defined with regard to their influence on the company's performance indicators: profitability and competitive advantage, which is directly related to system costs, including license fee, consultant expenses, maintenance cost and infrastructure cost. This system cost or price is a dimension that determines a company's competitive advantage and is calculated as the total amount of expenses related to ERP implementation. Moon [MOO 07] explained that since the investment and collective efforts required to implement and run ERP systems are significant to any organization, the fundamental question of the ERP system's value has been a key issue: is an ERP system of any value to an organization? What values can an ERP system bring to an organization? The value assessment methods can be numerous and complex. For example, the benefits may be measured by cost savings, return on investment, asset turnover, return on assets, and perceptions by the market, etc.

An ERP system helps different parts of an organization to share data and reduce costs [ALA 01]. The promised benefits of a successful ERP implementation appear attractive to an organization, because they include reductions in costs (inventory, raw materials and production), customer lead times and production times [SOM 01]. Companies that automate and streamline workflows across multiple sites (including suppliers, partners and manufacturing sites) produced 66% more improvement in reducing total time from order to delivery (Aberdeen's 2007 study of the role of ERP in globalization). There are also reports of ERP systems providing benefits such as cost reductions, improved productivity, better managerial decision-making and facilitation of process or structural change [SHA 00, BAR 02, KAM 08, FED 09].

However, Majed [ALM 00] reported that 70% of ERP implementations did not achieve their estimated benefits. Companies must be competitive to sell their goods and services in the marketplace. A research note has published the results of an analysis of 81 public companies that use systems, applications and products for data processing (SAP) software and were listed on SAP's Website. Contrary to SAP's advertising claim that "Best run Businesses run SAP" and that its customers are 32% more profitable than their peers, SAP customers were in fact 20% less profitable than their peers. SAP customers had an average "return on equity (ROE)" of 12.6% versus an industry average of 15.7%. It is interesting to note that some areas of significant focus for SAP, customer relationship management (CRM) and supply chain management (SCM) had customers who fared quite poorly, with CRM customers achieving 18% lower profitability and SCM customers achieving 40% lower profitability than their peers [CAM 06].

Should the competitiveness of a firm, especially within the context of economic crisis, be a criterion to be taken into account by all stakeholders within the framework of an ERP's evolution? If so, would IS integration be favored? If not, would its disintegration be provoked? In other words, could the economic crisis lead firms to avoid an ERP system's selection because of its high costs? If so, could this crisis delay IS integration or even promote its disintegration?

Generally, an integrated IS is an important element contributing to the firm's competitiveness. Depending on the ROI of the ERP system, this contribution could be positive or negative. While faced with economic crisis, firms' arbitration (via the ROI) in terms of ERP projects is crucial. It allows firms to make important decisions regarding the adoption of ERP systems (or not) as part of their IS.

Consequently, if the competitiveness of firms could be improved by an ERP system, the integration rate of IS would be increased. On the contrary, if the competitiveness of firms could not be improved by the selection of an ERP system or even by its expansion from 1st G to 2nd G, a kind of IS disintegration would be maintained or even increased. As a result, we can propose economic crisis and competitiveness (ECCO) as a factor that could guide the relationship between the ERP system's evolution and IS integration or disintegration.

Based on an exploration of the literature, as well as a logical analysis and the rating schema suggested in our research methodology, we assign this factor, within the context of economic crisis, two different values (one positive and another negative): if the competitiveness would be improved by an ERP system (as evidenced by a positive arbitration of ROI), the value "ECCO+" is given; whereas, if competitiveness could not be improved by an ERP system (as evidenced by a negative arbitration of ROI), the value "ECCO–" will be assigned.

As an ERP system is a element favoring IS integration, we think that an "ECCO+" could promote a total integration of IS (TIIS) or an hybrid integration of IS (HIIS) (e.g. the IS would be totally integrated if the architecture is composed of one ERP system only, which can improve the firm's competitiveness; while the IS would be more or less integrated if the ERP system that helps to increase this competitiveness is only a part, with other applications, of the IS). However, we believe that an "ECCO-" could encourage an HIIS or even a disintegrated information system (DIS) (e.g. the IS would be partially integrated if, instead of an ERP system's expansion from 1st to 2nd G, which does not improve the firm's competitiveness, a part of the ERP 1st G is completed by some "Best of Breed (BoB)" applications, which are more or less integrated with this ERP system; or if the firm keeps its disintegrated legacy systems without any selection of an ERP system due to a negative arbitration of ROI).

4.2. Total dependency on the ERP vendor (TDEV)

"Do customers want to keep the freedom to choose the best solution for each application domain?" [LAM 01]. Among firms deploying ERP systems, very few adopt all the available process modules, opting not to be fully committed to the integration and standardization options required by the ERP system [THE 01, ROW 05, BID 12]. Independent ERP consultants should be impartial when assessing their technology level, because ERP vendors or implementation specialists tend to favor their own production features [RAT 12].

ERP modularity is analyzed by Kumar *et al.* [KUM 02, KUM 03], Bueno and Salmeron [BUE 08] and Ratkevičius [RAT 12]. Modularity enables ERP customers from all available functionalities to choose modules and functional groups that are necessary for their organization. Our definition of the dependency on the ERP vendor matches with the definition of ERP modularity. Total dependency means that the company is obliged to buy all of the modules of an ERP (complete package) without being able to acquire only some modules (independence). The total dependence on the ERP vendor (or a reduced number of vendors) could be seen by companies in two different ways:

– a desire for such dependence, which allows the firm to have a limited number of counterparts related to IS (advantage);

– a fear of such dependence, which means that a vendor is in a position of power and influence over the company (disadvantage).

The current policy that has been adopted by vendors is often a policy of independence given to firms to choose the modules that meet their needs and desires. Firms are under no obligation to purchase the complete package (all modules). "At Oracle we prefer the term "E-Business Suite" to that of "integrated whole". It is our way to explain that we do not impose on our customers to immediately buy all of our products when they are only interested in a single brick. Our approach is very modular" [ANI 01]. SAP R/3 reaches a high level of variability and flexibility (modularity) by allowing customers to select only those modules that are required for their specific business scenario [UFL 07]. We note that the factor of the dependency on the ERP vendor is taken into consideration by Oracle and SAP.

Should the dependency of a firm on vendors be a criterion to be taken into account by all stakeholders within the framework of an ERP system's evolution? If so, would IS integration be improved? If not, would its disintegration be initiated?

Consequently, we propose the total dependency on the ERP vendor (TDEV) as a factor that could guide and affect the relationship between the ERP system's evolution and IS integration or disintegration. In fact, a total dependency on one ERP vendor promotes the integration of IS (e.g. the IS would be totally integrated [TIIS] if it is composed of only one ERP); while, an independence from one ERP vendor helps develop a kind of disintegration (e.g. the IS would be more or less integrated [HIIS] if it is composed of many ERP systems that are interconnected or the IS would be disintegrated [DIS] if the architecture is composed of many subsystems [ERP systems, applications, etc.] that are not interconnected).

Based on an exploration of the literature, as well as a logical analysis and the rating schema suggested in our research methodology, we assign this factor two different values (one positive and another negative): total dependency on the ERP vendor "TDEV+" or independence from the ERP vendor "TDEV-". As an ERP system is a factor favoring IS integration, we think that a "TDEV+" could promote a TIIS, while a "TDEV-" could encourage an HIIS or even a DIS.

4.3. Project management ERP (PMER)

Some researchers have investigated factors (e.g. top management support, sufficient training, proper project management, communication, etc.) that are critical to the success of ERP implementation [BIN 99, GRI 99, HOL 99, KUM 00, WIL 00, HON 02, VER 02]. Yang *et al.* [YAN 07] mention the importance of the service quality of consultants (expertise about ERP implementation, ability of project manager, implementation methodology and tool, and experience on similar cases).

Several researchers have also mentioned the importance of suitable customization (parameterization possibilities): [MAB 00, KUM 03, BER 05, YAN 07]. Reliable management of an ERP project should be based on good customization, adequacy of user training, competency in project implementation team, acceptance of changes brought about by implementation and support and participation of external consultants [CHE 08b]. As an ERP system is an element favoring IS integration, a relationship between the CSFs in ERP implementations and IS integration could be proposed.

Although the success factors of ERP projects are frequently analyzed and their impacts on IS integration are emphasized, the role of failure factors is not sufficiently studied as an eventual stimulator of IS disintegration. "Many ERP systems still face resistance, and ultimately, failure" [ALA 01]. "Failure rates are estimated to be as high as 50% of all ERP implementations" [MUS 06]. "70 percent of ERP implementations fail to deliver anticipated benefits" [WAN 07]. Despite the promise of ERP applications, studies have found that a high percentage of ERP implementations are classified as failures [WON 03, HIC 10, KAN 11]. Panorama Consulting predicted an increase in the number of ERP failures and lawsuits for 2012 [KIM 11].

Many authors have studied risks in ERP projects, and several risk categories have been proposed. By making a synthesis of the propositions of Aloini *et al.*, Barki *et al.*, Bourdeau *et al.*, Bradford *et al.*, Bradley, Kyung-Kwon *et al.*, Tiwana *et al.*, Tsai *et al.* and Weiling *et al.* [ALO 07, BAR 93, BOU 03, BRA 03, BRA 08, KYU 02, TIW 06, TSA 09c, WEI 08], the project risk categories are: – stopping the project; – overrunning the deadline and exceeding the budget; – degree of integration desired is not reached; –

lack of overall vision; – lack of project team's skills (internal and/or external); – resistance to change by users; – inadequate business project reengineering (BPR); – inadequate training and instruction; – gap between specific needs and generic processes provided by the ERP; – a lot of specific developments; – poor settings (configuration); – project complexity, which can be linked to the ERP complexity.

Davenport [DAV 98] attributed many failures of ERP implementation to a lack of alignment with business needs. There is no single "best process" to do business, as ERP systems assume, and, therefore, the customization of ERP systems is necessary. He further cautioned that firms could lose their source of advantage by adopting processes that are indistinguishable from those of their competitors. However, aligning the business process to the software implementation is critical because, as far as possible, software should not be modified [HOL 99, SUM 99]. Modifications should be avoided to reduce errors and to take advantage of newer releases [ROS 00]. "You should never go too far in the specific (developed programs), otherwise you lose the whole point of a package" [GAU 07]. A lot of specific coding could make the ERP lose the advantages of integration.

Unreliable management of an ERP project is the result of bad customization, lack of user training, absence of in-house skills and deficiency of project team expertise [AND 79, BAR 93, HOL 99, JIA 99]. As an ERP system is a factor of IS integration, a relationship between the CFFs in ERP implementations and IS disintegration could be proposed.

Should a methodology for optimizing project management, based on best practices, be a criterion to be taken into account by all stakeholders within the framework of an ERP system's evolution? If so, would IS integration be improved? If not, would its disintegration be possible?

Consequently, there is a relationship between the CSF/CFF in ERP implementations and IS integration or disintegration. We propose the "Project Management ERP (PMER)" as a factor that could guide and impact the relationship between the ERP system's evolution and IS integration or disintegration. As an ERP system is a factor favoring IS integration, the success of ERP project management promotes IS integration, which would consist of well-implemented ERP system; while the failure of ERP project management can lead to a kind of IS disintegration (the ERP system would not be well implemented and would not be well integrated within the framework of the whole architecture). We are interested in the failure of an ERP system's implementation because we think that it could engender a kind of regression from a TIIS to an HIIS or to a DIS.

Based on an exploration of the literature, as well as a logical analysis and the rating schema suggested in the research methodology, we assign this factor two different values (one positive and another negative): reliable ERP project management "PMER+" or unreliable "PMER-". We think that a "PMER+" could promote a TIIS or an HIIS, while a "PMER-" could encourage a DIS.

4.4. INTEroperability of the ERP (INTE)

"Interoperability is the connectivity of two systems to flow information freely from one to another and back again" [JAM 05]. Indeed, interoperability is characterized by the ability of independent systems to work together with minimal effort [KON 05]. It is also the capacity for two systems to understand one another and to use functionality of one another [CHE 08a]. The word "inter-operate" implies that one system performs an operation for another system. Precisely, "it is the ability of information systems, and the business processes they support, to exchange data and enable sharing of information" [PAP 03].

The interoperability of an ERP system is its ability to interact with other subsystems (applications, legacy systems, ERP systems, etc.) within the whole of the IS. The interoperability allows us to evaluate the ERP software suitability, which could be evaluated by the integration possibilities of an ERP system whose software is already in use. This kind of opinion is held by Everdingen *et al.*, Sprott, Kumar *et al.*, Verville and Halingten, Fisher and Kiang, Bueno and Salmeron and Ratkevičius *et al.* [EVE 00, SPR 00, KUM 02, KUM 03, VER 03, FIS 04, BUE 08, RAT 12]. For the purpose of our research, we are not interested in the native interoperability between the modules of an ERP system that should be reliable according to ERP's founding principles and definition. We are interested rather in the interoperability between the ERP system and other subsystems within the whole IS.

Today, there are different technologies that lead to the improvement of the interoperability within an IS. Interfaces for commercial software applications or legacy systems within an ERP suite may need to be developed in-house if they are not available in the market [BIN 99]. New integration technology such as software componentization, enterprise application integration (EAI), service-oriented architecture (SOA) and Web Services are introduced and their implications are discussed [MOO 07]. In spite of this need for coexistence between the subsystems, ERP packages are not designed to be incorporated into existing systems [SCH 00]. A survey from 2009 remarks that eight of 10 users cite a significant need for improvement in interoperability [MCG 09]. As a result, for the purpose of our research, we suggest two types of ERP interoperability: reliable or unreliable.

Should improving interoperability be a criterion to be taken into account by all stakeholders within the framework of an ERP system's evolution? If so, would the IS integration be improved? If not, would its disintegration be initiated?

Logically, a reliable interoperability can promote the integration of different subsystems within the IS (e.g. an incomplete ERP 2nd G, which does not contain all modules but whose interoperability is reliable, could be easily interfaced with a part of the legacy systems. As a result, there is good communication between the modules of this package and the rest of the architecture. In this case, the IS would be more or less integrated [HIIS]); while, an unreliable interoperability leads to a kind of disintegration between the different subsystems (e.g. an ERP 1st G, whose interoperability is unreliable, which could not be interfaced with other applications within the IS. As a result, there is no communication between the modules of this package and the rest of the architecture. In this case, the IS would rather be disintegrated [DIS]). Consequently, we propose the "INTEroperability of the ERP (INTE)" as a factor that could guide and impact the relationship between the ERP system's evolution and IS integration or disintegration.

Based on an exploration of the literature, as well as a logical analysis and the rating schema suggested in our research methodology, we assign this factor two different values (one positive and another negative): reliable interoperability of the ERP "INTE+" or unreliable interoperability of the ERP "INTE-". As an ERP is a factor favoring IS integration, we think that an "INTE+" could promote an HIIS, while an "INTE-" could encourage a DIS. Contradictorily, we think that an "INTE-" could sometimes lead to a TIIS (e.g. because of the lack of the ERP system's interoperability, the firm avoids interfacing any other subsystem with the ERP system to implement. In this case, the IS would consist only of this ERP system, and a total overhaul of the existing system would be necessary. This idea will be explained in the next section).

4.5. Evolution strategy of existing systems (ESES)

The evolution strategy of existing systems (IT strategy) is managed by firms to implement an information system that serves their business process in the short term and their corporate strategies in the long term. It represents the business vision and IT strategies, as expressed in business strategies and visions. The target must be able to serve the strategy and business process within an IS that is aligned with corporate strategy.

When the ESES is based on ERP implementation, it aims to evaluate the fit of the ERP system in relation to the underlying business strategy. The state of the existing system could determine a firm's ESES. ERP implementation involves a complex transition from legacy IS and business processes to an integrated IT infrastructure and common business processes throughout the organization [GIB 99]. Verville and Harlington emphasize the compatibility between an ERP implementation and the existing system: "is the organization's existing DBMS compatible with the proposed solution and can the proposed solution integrate into the organization's existing hardware architecture" [VER 03].

One of the main functions of an ESES is auditing the state of the existing system, which helps to set the objectives and strategy of the target. In order to reach this target and to evolve the existing systems, firms can principally chose one of two different strategies: urbanization or total overhaul.

4.5.1. *Urbanization*

The model of information system development has changed since the mid-1990s, with a move toward so-called urbanization, where systems are constructed from existing applications and new systems [HOP 08]. This strategy is based on modernizing and judiciously profiting from technological advances without erasing the past while continuing business operations while the work is carried out [LON 09]. Urbanization is the implementation of an ERP system without erasing all of the legacy systems (e.g. a functional part of legacy systems would within the IS would remain intact). The integration of the subsystems is one of the founding principles of the urbanization according to its definition.

Urbanization, which is a French framework of enterprise architecture (EA), is a process that makes an IS more suitable for serving the corporate strategy and anticipating changes in business environment [CIG 03]. The concept involves reconstructing the IS based on permanent components. It consists of moving from an existing IT system to a target one by successive stepwise stages, whereas a total overhaul is considered a more radical approach. Some firms, such as Air France KLM, Renault and BNP Paribas, have found urbanization to be an advantageous approach [TRA 13].

Consequently, urbanization consists of evolving the IS by keeping the part of the existing IS that is functional and operational. For example: urbanizing by expanding the IS's perimeter from an ERP 1st G to an ERP 2nd G. This kind of urbanization could lead to a TIIS when both packages (ERP 1st G and ERP 2nd G) are bought from the same vendor; the urbanization is managed by adding and interfacing other third-party subsystems (applications and/or software packages) to an ERP 1st G. This kind of urbanization could lead to an HIIS instead, especially when the subsystems (Best of Breed or not) are sold by many software vendors.

4.5.2. *Total overhaul*

A whole replacement of all legacy systems with another at one time is termed in France a "Total Overhaul", which involves making a clean sweep in order to completely replace the existing system by a new IS. For example, old applications developed in-house are completely replaced by an ERP 2nd G or by many interfaced subsystems (ERP systems and/or others).

The choice of a given strategy (total overhaul or urbanization) depends on the state of the existing system (extremely complex, complex or simple). "If an organization's legacy systems are extremely complex, with multiple technology platforms and a variety of procedures to manage common business processes, then the amount of technical and organizational change required is high. Otherwise, if the organization already has a simple technical architecture, change requirements are low" [HOL 99].

Generally, firms prefer urbanization over total overhaul, which is costly, time-consuming and difficult to achieve. Unfortunately, many organizations have faced a challenge with systems integration related to the complexity of existing systems, which in many cases have fixed and rigid structures for messages, interfaces and databases [THE 02]. As a result, a total overhaul sometimes may be indispensable, especially when the existing system is very complex.

Yang *et al.* [YAN 07] have mentioned the importance of the compatibility and adaptability of an ERP system with existing systems (employed system technologies, embedded database system, system development tool and language). When compatibility and adaptability are completely absent, the only remaining option when selecting an ERP system is to adopt a total overhaul, because urbanization would be very difficult to manage and a favorable result would be much less likely. The more complex the existing system is, the more difficult the urbanization is; the simpler the existing system, the easier it would be to avoid a total overhaul in favor of urbanization.

Should the firm's evolution strategy of existing systems be a criterion to be taken into account by all stakeholders within the framework of the ERP system's evolution? If so, would IS integration be improved? If not, would its disintegration be provoked?

Logically, a total overhaul could improve IS integration, especially where the legacy systems are extremely complex (e.g. the implementation of an ERP 2nd G, by a total overhaul, could lead to a "TIIS"; likewise, a total overhaul leading to an ERP 1st G that is well interfaced with many "BoB" applications could lead to an HIIS). However, urbanization performed on a simple or sometimes on a complex existing system could lead to an "HIIS" or a "DIS" instead of a "TIIS" (e.g. an urbanization performed on a simple existing system that leads to an ERP system that is well integrated with the existing system promotes an "HIIS"; while urbanization executed on a complex existing system that leads to an ERP system that is not at all integrated with the existing systems could lead to a DIS instead). The only case for which urbanization could lead to a TIIS is when the firm migrates an ERP 1st G to an ERP 2nd G that was bought from the same vendor.

As a result, we propose the "Evolution Strategy of Existing Systems (ESES)" as a factor that could guide and impact the relationship between the ERP system's evolution and IS integration or disintegration. Based on an exploration of the literature, as well as a logical analysis and the rating schema suggested in our research methodology, we assign this factor two different values (one positive and another negative): a total overhaul performed, especially, on an extremely complex existing system would be positive "ESES+", while urbanization performed on a simple or a complex existing system would be negative "ESES–". We think that an "ESES+" could promote a TIIS or an HIIS, while an "ESES–" could lead to an HIIS or a DIS more than a TIIS, which can happen in only one scenario (i.e. urbanization from an ERP 1st G to an ERP 2nd G bought from the same vendor).

4.6. Complexity of ERP (COER)

Different approaches for measuring software complexity are discussed in the related literature. Very often, ERP system buyers focus on ERP system price and its functionality without considering the IT skills of future users [RAT 12]. Ease of use is often an undervalued ERP system selection criterion according to Pivnicny and Carmody, Everdingen, Verville and Halingten, Yang *et al.*, and Bueno and Salmeron [PIV 89, EVE 00, VER 03, YAN 07, BUE 08]. Wei *et al.* define it as a measure of the simplicity of training and use [WEI 05]. Keil and Tiwana treat this criterion as the possibility for using the software intuitively, without additional specific knowledge [KEI 06]. An ERP system requires the collaboration and understanding of people across the entire organization. After implementation of a complex ERP, demotivated users may avoid using it and try to replace some functions of the software package by other tools. This behavior, which can be related to a lack of training and experience, does not encourage an integrated way of working.

ERP implementation is a lengthy and complex process [PAR 00]. It is generally accepted that ERP systems are complex systems involving not only technical aspects but also business processes. ERP systems have frequently been criticized for being rigid, massive and consequently hard to implement and control [CIB 00, HAN 01]. The selection of an ERP system is a difficult and long-term process; an organization must choose a supplier capable of providing a flexible ERP system [SPR 00, EVE 00, SHE 04, WEI 04].

Uflacker and Busse mentioned the difficulty of performing a desired business task using SAP [UFL 07]. They used the term "front-end complexity" to qualify the underlying program, and "back-end complexity" to mean the difficulty of use as perceived by the end user: the flexible and holistic approach of SAP R/3 introduces a considerable amount of functional complexity into the "Sales and Distribution module SD" (the authors illustrate enterprise application complexity by analyzing sales order management and order variations in SAP). "So is SAP complicated? Of course it is," said Christian Hestermann, an analyst at Gartner [ROB 11].

Should simplifying the complexity be a criterion to be taken into account by all stakeholders within the framework of ERP system's evolution? If so, would IS integration be improved? If not, would its disintegration be possible?

When a complex ERP system is selected and implemented by firms, the IS integration may be compromised (e.g. a complex ERP system would be difficult to use or may be used incorrectly in a manner that spreads incorrect data within the IS, thereby rendering the integration useless or devoid of any added value). However, when a simple ERP system (as opposed to a complex one) is adopted by firms, IS integration could be improved (e.g. a simple ERP system could be used easily and correctly in a manner that spreads accurate data within the IS, thereby leading to a useful integration).

As a result, we propose "COmplexity of ERP (COER)" as a factor that could guide and impact the relationship between the ERP system's evolution and IS integration or disintegration. Based on an exploration of the literature, as well as a logical analysis and the rating schema suggested in our research methodology, we assign this factor two different values (one positive and another negative): simple ERP system would be positive "COER+" vs. a complex ERP system, which would be negative "COER−". We think that a "COER+" could promote a TIIS as well as an HIIS, while a "COER−" could lead to a DIS instead.

4.7. Evolution strategy of ERP vendors (ESEV)

ERP packages do not seem to be able to "cover all the business processes of an enterprise" [SCH 00]. "To best meet business needs, companies may integrate other specialized software products with the ERP suite" [BIN 99]. Functional match is a measure of the strength and capability of the ERP system to meet the business requirements of the firm [LAL 06]. A major problem with the existing ERP systems is the misfit between the delivered functionality from the vendor and the needed functionality in the receiving end-customer organization. This has led to an increasing interest among vendors to improve future ERP systems to support the end-customer organization even better [JOH 07].

Vendors are required to demonstrate how their ERP systems meet the functionalities identified by the company. Firms that have already implemented ERP systems and are relatively satisfied with their operations are now considering the extension of the functionalities provided by the original ERP systems. Some companies implement ERP systems even though their ultimate objectives lie in further extended systems. Others implement ERP systems with some plans to extend later. Consequently, enlarging the ERP system's perimeter (scope) from 1st G toward 2nd G, which takes into account new modules such as business intelligence (BI), CRM, SCM, etc., could fit better with the new users' needs and improve IS integration.

ERP package functionalities are one of the most important software-related ERP system selection criteria. It could be evaluated by taking into account the standard functional power and its suitability to company needs. This factor was mentioned in the research papers of Everdingen *et al.*, Siriginidi, Chen, Kumar *et al.*, Wei *et al.*, Keil and Tiwana, Liao *et al.* and others [EVE 00, SIR 00a, CHE 01, KUM 02, KUM 03, WEI 05, KEI 06, LIA 07]. Anderson and Chen treat ERP system functionality as the main ERP system selection criterion [AND 97]. Heck presents a similar opinion, affirming that this criterion must comprise up to one-third of the final score used for making the ERP system selection decision [HEC 97].

In Kumar's survey of Canadian companies, functionality has been the most often quoted and the most important ERP system selection factor to consider, mentioned in 79% of the cases [KUM 03]. Han has analyzed ERP system functionality as a unique and as the main significant ERP system selection criterion, separating three levels of system functionality [HAN 04]. The first one includes the basic system functionality and the third level provides an additional ERP functionality that extends the limits of collected and processed information (for example, ensuring real-time communication between customers and suppliers). ERP functionality could be used as a reference point to prioritize the performed functions as one of the principal ERP system selection strategies [RAT 12].

Researchers also investigate the importance of ERP system vendor reputation. This criterion has been cited in the research papers of Kumar *et al.*, Verville and Halingten, Wei *et al.*, Lall and Teyarachakul, and Liao *et al.* [KUM 02, KUM 03, VER 03, WEI 05, LAL 06, LIA 07]. The vendor reputation, technical capabilities and provision of ongoing services need to be considered in the ERP system vendor selection process.

Vendor reputation is defined as one of the most important non-technical ERP selection criteria [BRO 81, CHA 95]. Goldenberg *et al.* and Pivnicny and Carmody treat vendor reputation as the only factor that requires consideration [GOL 91, PIV 89]. Bernroider and Koch have indicated that this factor is more significant for large than for small- or mid-sized companies [BER 01]. A definition of ERP system vendor reputation has been introduced by Verveille and Hallinten [VER 03], and it highlights vendor recognition, as well as technological and strategic vision.

A long-lasting perspective of ERP system vendor existence is also an important ERP system selection criterion. Many researchers and practitioners hold the opinion that a long-lasting perspective of ERP system vendor existence is the prerequisite to ensuring and developing the actual ERP system functionality from the perspective of new business trends.

Rao identified some ERP system selection criteria for Indian small- and medium-sized enterprises (SMEs): domain knowledge suppliers, uses latest technology and upgrade ability, which characterizes the ability of the ERP system vendor to upgrade the current ERP system to a newer version [RAO 00]. The importance of the upgrade ability is also mentioned by Sprott, Kumar *et al.*, and Bueno and Salmeron [SPR 00, KUM 02, KUM 03, BUE 08]. Vendor profile is an attribute based on prompt availability of software upgrades and technical support [LAL 06].

Advanced technology of ERP system vendors is also an important but not crucial ERP system selection criterion. This factor is described in detail by Rao and Kumar *et al.* [RAO 00, KUM 02, KUM 03]. When selecting an ERP system by this criterion, the ERP system's technological architecture, its structure, database, programming platform administration possibilities, workflows, document management and report generation tools are evaluated.

To summarize, Liao *et al.* [LIA 07] provide four ERP system selection criteria: function and technology, strategic fitness, vendor ability and vendor reputation. All these criteria could be taken into account to define the research factor "Evolution Strategy of ERP Vendors from 1st to 2nd G (ESEV)," as also shown in Table 4.1.

The observation of the ERP system vendors' market allows us to define three main strategies:

1) to stop an activity at the level of ERP 1st G because the vendor is bought out by another ERP system vendor (e.g. PeopleSoft and J.D. Edwards);

2) to maintain the perimeter at the level "1st G" without any expansion toward an ERP 2nd G;

3) to extend the ERP 1st G's perimeter by adding new modules, by internal development (e.g. SAP) or by acquisition of other ERP system vendors (e.g. Oracle).

"In 1998 there were five major software vendors offering ERP solutions to businesses worldwide. The largest of these was SAP AG. The Oracle Corp. was the second, followed in third place by PeopleSoft. In fourth place was J.D. Edwards. Finally in fifth place was the Baan Co" [HOL 99]. Today, this situation has changed because PeopleSoft and J.D. Edwards, considered ERP 1st G, have stopped their activities due to being purchased by Oracle. This "Stopping Business" strategy can impact the IS because some firms still keep PeopleSoft and/or J.D. Edwards as a subset within their architectures.

Oracle has preferred an external acquisition strategy, rather than internal development, to obtain indispensable know-how to evolve and optimize certain modules in its ERP 2nd G. "This logic of buyout is to take ownership of another vendor for its expertise in a particular module" [PRA 08]. It seems that an external acquisition strategy does not allow a vendor to develop its ERP 2nd G on the founding principles of a total integration "TIIS", as shown in Table 1.1.

It also seems that it is very difficult for one vendor to have all the necessary knowledge and competencies in all modules of an ERP 2nd G. This could mean that there is a doubt about the reliability of an ERP 2nd G sold by a vendor that adopted an internal development strategy to optimize its software package. As a result, this book does not aim to judge which ERP system is more reliable than another (obtained by internal development or external acquisition). Instead, it focuses on the integration rate that – in our belief – is not the only element that determines the reliability of an IS.

Consequently, when an internal development strategy is adopted by an ERP system vendor, the integration rate of the IS would be improved (e.g. the implementation of an ERP 2nd G SAP could lead to a "TIIS" especially when the whole architecture consists only of SAP modules); while, when an external acquisition strategy is utilized by an ERP system vendor, the IS would be more or less integrated (e.g. the implementation of an Oracle ERP 2nd G could lead to an "HIIS").

However, if the ERP system evolution is stopped at the level of ERP 1st G (the vendor is bought out by another ERP vendor; or perhaps the ERP system evolution is maintained at the level "1st G" without any expansion toward an ERP 2nd G), an IS disintegration could result (e.g. the perimeter of an IS that consists only of an ERP PeopleSoft 1st G is enlarged to an IS that now consists of an ERP PeopleSoft 1st G with some other applications such as CRM, SCM, etc.). In this example, the reliability of the IS integration could depend on the integration rate within the IS:

– an unreliable integration between all these subsystems could lead to a kind of strong disintegration from a "TIIS" (when the IS in the past consisted only of PeopleSoft 1st G) to a "DIS" (if the other applications have not recently been integrated with PeopleSoft 1st G);

– while a reliable integration between all these subsystems could encourage a kind of weak disintegration from a "TIIS" (when the IS in the past consisted only of PeopleSoft 1st G) to an "HIIS" (if the other applications have recently been well integrated with PeopleSoft 1st G).

Should the evolution strategy of ERP system vendors from 1st to 2nd G be a criterion to be taken into account by all stakeholders within the framework of an ERP system's evolution? If so, would the IS integration be improved? If not, would it result in disintegration?

We propose the "Evolution Strategy of ERP Vendors from 1st to 2nd G (ESEV)" as a factor that could guide and impact the relationship between the ERP system's evolution and IS integration or disintegration.

Based on an exploration of the literature review, as well as a logical analysis and the rating schema suggested in our research methodology, we assign this factor two different values (one positive and another negative): evolution to an ERP 2nd G by internal development or external acquisition would be positive "ESEV+," while keeping an ERP 1st G without any expansion toward a 2nd G or by the vendor going out of business would be negative "ESEV–". We can also distinguish two degrees within the framework of the positive value "ESEV+".

– a high positive value could be attributed when the expansion strategy to an ERP 2nd G is achieved by internal development;

– a low positive value could be given when the expansion strategy used to transition to an ERP 2nd G was external acquisition.

As an ERP is a factor favoring IS integration, we think that an "ESEV+" could promote a TIIS, or an HIIS, while an "ESEV-" could cause a disintegration toward an HIIS or even toward a DIS.

This chapter highlighted the seven research factors that we determined affect the relationships between the ERP system's evolution and IS integration or disintegration. Each of these factors is a variable that could be defined by two different values (+ or -). Each of these two values could differently affect the IS evolution (integration or disintegration). We have evaluated the research factors according to the definitions below.

Research's factors	Values	Evaluations (ratings)
Economic crisis and competitiveness	*ECCO +*	Competitiveness would be improved due to an ERP (a positive arbitration of ROI)
	ECCO -	Competitiveness could not be improved due to an ERP (a negative arbitration of ROI)
Total dependency on the ERP vendor	*TDEV +*	Total dependency on the ERP vendor
	TDEV -	Independence from the ERP vendor
Project management ERP	*PMER +*	Reliable ERP project management
	PMER -	Unreliable ERP project management
INTEroperability of the ERP	*INTE +*	Reliable interoperability of the ERP
	INTE -	Unreliable interoperability of the ERP
Evolution strategy of existing systems	*ESES +*	Total overhaul performed, especially, on extremely complex existing
	ESES -	Urbanization performed on a simple or a complex existing
COmplexity of ERP	*COER +*	Simple ERP
	COER -	Complex ERP
Evolution strategy of ERP vendors	*ESEV +*	Evolution to an ERP 2nd G by an internal development or by an external acquisition
	ESEV -	Keeping an ERP 1st G without any expansion toward a 2nd G or by the vendor going out of business

Table 4.2. *Measurement of the research factors affecting the relationships between the ERP system's evolution and IS integration or disintegration*

5

Correlation Between Research Factors

This chapter studies the correlation between research factors. Based on the literature review and a logical deduction, we explored potential relationships between the research factors. Once relationships were illustrated, we assessed and determined the nature of the correlations between these factors. A correlation is the measurement of the relationship between two variables or more. We define two principal types of correlations: *"positive correlation"* (PC) is a direct relationship where, as the amount of one variable (factor) increases, the amount of a second variable also increases; *"negative correlation"* (NC) describes a relationship where, as the amount of one variable goes up, the amount of another variable goes down.

The study of the above research factors raised some questions to explore, for example:

– Could the Project management ERP (PMER) be easy if the enterprise resource planning (ERP) package is a complex product?

– Could a desired independence from the vendor (guaranteed by ERP package modularity) be affected by the lack of the interoperability of the ERP (INTE)?

– Would a total overhaul strategy be less expensive during a period of economic crisis and competitiveness (ECCO)?

– Could the competitiveness of firms within the framework of an economic crisis be affected by the total dependency on the ERP vendors (TDEV)?

– Would an evolution strategy of ERP system vendors from 1st to 2nd G that is based on an external acquisition decrease the return on investment (ROI) because of difficulties in updating and upgrading the system?

– Would an evolution strategy of ERP system vendors that is based on internal development affect the firm's competitiveness because of the potential unreliability of some modules?

According to Ayağ and Özdemi [AYA 07], ERP system selection criteria may be classified into seven dimensions and 22 criteria. All criteria of one dimension are connected and influence each other either positively or negatively. Productivity directly correlates with the system's support efficiency. Profitability influences more than half (13 out of 22) of the criteria mentioned in their research paper (upgrade possibility, ease of integration, ease of in-house development, functionality, module completion, function fitness, security level, reliability, stability, possibility of recovery, ease of use, ease of operations, ease of learning, technology advance, standardization and integration of legacy systems).

We will first explore the general correlations between many factors, followed by an analysis of potential correlations between any two factors, as explained in the following sections.

5.1. Correlations between economic crisis and competitiveness (ECCO) and PMER and INTE and COER

The complexity of selecting an ERP package can add a lot of time to the ERP system project (Computer Technology Research Corporation 1999). In the mid-1990s, systems, applications and products for data processing (SAP) generated a significant amount of negative publicity claiming that SAP was too expensive, too complicated and took too long to implement. There has been an ongoing effort for over a decade to add a greater level of simplicity to SAP deployments. The complexity of ERP (COER), high costs and implementation problems force numerous organizations to reconsider their new plans in relation to this enterprise system [KUM 00]. According to [CAR 04]:

> "Customizing the already complex ERP created yet more complexity and even larger risks. Without intimate knowledge of how the integrated pieces of these modular software packages

actually worked, customizing could lead to in-house bugs and glitches that were hard to foresee and expensive to fix".

Most ERP packages are very complex systems, so interfacing with these systems is not an easy task. Testing the links between ERP packages and other corporate software links that have to be built on a case-by-case basis is another time- and cost-consuming project task [LEO 07]. The total costs of ownership and deployment time are considerably increased by significant implementation efforts, business configuration and customization complexity [UFL 07]. Challenges with solution complexity and cost continue to be an issue, according to Christian Hestermann, an analyst at Gartner [ROB 11].

5.2. Correlations between ECCO and PMER and INTE and ESEV

Different manufacturers of ERP packages are developing common integrated solutions helping to integrate different systems quickly and cost-efficiently [RAT 12]. This kind of partnership is supported by scientists who consider systems integration to be one of the three most problematic areas of ERP implementation [THE 01], strongly related to the success of the whole project [BIN 99]. Most companies will have some system that will not fit into the functionality of ERP packages and that will have to be interfaced with the ERP package.

Today, the functionality of universal and modern ERP systems includes almost all standardized business processes. However, in some cases, the activity area of a company is unique and cannot be satisfied by an ERP system. In these cases, the implementation project must lead to integration between the ERP system and other systems already in use [RAT 12]. In order to meet a specific need, it is not advisable to program the ERP system with many specifically developed programs that prevent any reliable ERP system's evolution in the future, thereby making it difficult to interface with other subsystems.

5.3. Correlations between ECCO and PMER and COER and ESEV

"Perhaps customization of the already complex ERP made changing the software later, or upgrading to a newer version, far more difficult, and in some cases prohibitively expensive" [CAR 04]. The Evolution strategy of ERP vendors (ESEV) should take into account the ERP system's customization process, which is often complex and costly. According to Ayağ and Özdemir [AYA 07], ERP system functionality directly affects the company's productivity level and can be assessed by considering the complexity of the modules. The evolution strategy of ERP system vendors should lead to an ERP 2nd G for which the upgrading is not complex and is not costly.

5.4. Correlations between ECCO and TDEV and PMER

Modularity helps to significantly decrease ERP system implementation time and project costs, as firms pay only for the system features that will actually be used. Before making a decision about which standard and additional modules will be used, internal and external business processes should be analyzed [ZIA 06].

5.5. Correlations between ECCO and ESES and COER

Urbanization is essential to describe complex information systems (IS) and to develop standards that enable business competitiveness and flexibility. It is considered to be the way to understand and manage the complexity of an organization. It allows organizations to act and perform in increasingly dynamic environments [TRA 13].

5.6. Correlations between ECCO and ESES and ESEV

The assumption that an ERP system could improve firms' competitiveness requires the fulfillment of certain conditions:

– an expansion of the functional scope is to be implemented by the vendors to evolve an ERP system from 1st G to 2nd G. It is necessary to provide new modules (supply chain management (SCM), customer relationship management (CRM), e-business, etc.) that allow companies to improve their competitiveness and to reduce the costs with their partners;

– a strategy on the part of firms to accompany this expansion (urbanization or a total overhaul);

– an acceptable Total Cost of Ownership (TCO), which is crucial for firms.

5.7. Correlations between PMER and ESES and ESEV

The book has suggested various practices that are critical during the implementation of the ERP system. For example, almost every firm will discover inconsistencies between the ERP packages, current processes and organizational structure. Managers must determine whether they want to revise the ERP package or to adapt the current process and structure to the package [GRI 98]. The decision affects the implementation process and effectiveness of the ERP system.

5.8. Correlations between INTE and ESES and COER

Enterprise application integration (EAI) achieves internal data integration and can support process integration without replacement of legacy systems [IRA 03, SHA 05]. This allows a firm to retain legacy systems for some operations and keep extant production databases [BID 12]. Application programming interfaces (API) allow limited degrees of interoperability without requiring any formal architectural planning. In this approach, the individual application is king and the pragmatic need to connect at a superficial level requires the development and maintenance of software bridges linking application to application. Their development may be haphazard and may, over time, become a bricolage of programming. If the organization and its systems grow substantially, the complexity of maintaining these individual software APIs may overwhelm or force a move to other more formal or systematic integration approaches [BID 12].

For the purpose of our research, we reorganized and classified the literature describing the correlations between the research factors into the correlations between any two factors. Thus, the relationships between each pair of factors are studied below in more detail.

5.9. Correlation between ECCO and TDEV

In the case of a total dependency, the ERP system vendor could impose exaggerated financial conditions (consulting, maintenance and updates) that the company will not have the right to refuse or even to negotiate. For example, SAP has decided to abandon the initial rate of 17% (standard maintenance) and impose a single rate of 22% (enterprise support) on all customers. The majority of commentators use the word of "impose" to talk about this decision [FLE 08]. The good news accumulates for companies that have fallen into the SAP trap, dare I say SAP sect. Back in 2007, SAP had announced to all its customers a gradual increase in maintenance costs of 30% by 2012 [NAU 07].

In a situation of dependence, refusal of the vendor's conditions would mean that the firm may need to proceed to a difficult replacement of its ERP system. A refusal such as this may be explained by the fact that such an operation would be too expensive: "Increased dependency on ERP vendors and integrators is noted and recognized but freedom from ERP systems is difficult, long and painful. This is like a detox for alcoholics and for drug addicts or leaving a religious sect that selects new rich clients and rejects them when they are finally ruined" [NAU 07].

The ERP system's modularity (independence from the ERP vendor = TDEV–) could significantly decrease the system implementation costs (competitiveness would be improved due to an ERP system: a positive arbitration of ROI = ECCO+). The advantage to the ERP system vendor of the independence given to firms is the ability to better satisfy their budget. This allows the vendor to deal with clients without a large budget within the context of economic crisis.

Consequently, we can suggest a relative correlation between these two factors. It could be a positive correlation between TDEV– and ECCO+ (the more independent a firm is from an ERP system vendor, the more its competitiveness would increase due to an ERP system: a positive arbitration of ROI). However, we suggest a positive correlation between TDEV+ and ECCO– (the more dependent a firm is on an ERP system vendor, the more its competitiveness could not increase due to an ERP system: a negative arbitration of ROI).

5.10. Correlation between ECCO and PMER

Managing an ERP system project involves relatively large expenditures for the acquisition of the hardware, software, implementation, consulting and training [DAV 00, MCK 98], and can last for an extended period of time. ERP implementation projects are lengthy, and there have been many cases of unsuccessful implementations, which have had major impacts on business performance [PAR 00]. A survey conducted by "Panorama Consulting Group" (PCG) in 2011 found that ERP projects took longer than expected for 61% of the 185 surveyed companies, and costs exceeded budgets for 74% of these companies. More than half (53%) of the projects were reported to cost 189% of their original estimates [FIS 11].

Failure of ERP system implementation projects has been known to lead to problems as serious as organizational bankruptcy [BUL 96, DAV 98, MAR 00a]. There have been various definitions of failure of ERP implementation. Failure has been defined as an implementation that does not achieve a sufficient ROI identified in the project approval phase. Practitioners tend to discuss the impact of unreliable ERP project management (PMER–) in a relative sense, referring to the shutting down of the system, being able to use only part of the ERP system, suffering business loss, dropping market price, losing both market share and competitive advantage (ECCO–) due to implementation failure and so on [DEU 98, DIE 98, NEL 99].

ERP practitioners also give much attention to an inadequate analysis of ERP implementation costs. According to Langenwalter [LAN 00], ERP implementation projects fail in 40–60% of cases. Assessing an ROI of ERP software (ECCO–), the rate of unsuccessful projects (PMER–) becomes even higher 60–90% [PTA 00]. Leon [LEO 07] identified costs related to interruption possibilities and work efficiency fluctuations of internal staff members during the ERP project: trainings, brain drain (employee turnover) and ongoing maintenance. He also highlighted insufficiently identified costs related to an incorrect calculation of the direct amount of project work: customization, interaction and testing, data conversion and data analysis.

Though the cost of an ERP system is high, it becomes insignificant (ECCO+) compared to the benefits that a successful ERP implementation (PMER+) provides in the long run [SAD 99]. Consulting firms use techniques such as guided learning, formal training and knowledge creation activities to direct clients to the necessary knowledge required for a successful implementation. This guidance saves the client considerable time and effort in knowledge search costs [GAB 03].

Customizing an ERP system is also expensive. So, sticking to the basic configuration saves time and money. Some ERP system vendors propose solutions that are parameterized in advance using and classifying the most popular business processes by companies' size or industry. A reduction in customization time and efforts is achieved when the system is preconfigured

(PMER+) according to high-level characteristics of the customer organization. By offering such services to customers, vendors can significantly reduce the hurdle that is raised by purchase (ECCO+) and implementation costs [UFL 07]. According to Bueno and Salmeron [BUE 08], partly customized solutions significantly decrease the ERP system implementation period (PMER+) and system support costs (ECCO+).

As a result, we can suggest a relative correlation between these two factors. It could be a positive correlation between PMER+ and ECCO+ (the more reliable an ERP system's project management is, the more competitiveness would increase due to an ERP: a positive arbitration of ROI). However, we suggest a positive correlation between PMER– and ECCO– (the more unreliable an ERP system's project management is, the more competitiveness could not increase due to an ERP: a negative arbitration of ROI).

5.11. Correlation between ECCO and INTE

According to Hillestad *et al.* [HIL 05], the multi-level interoperability (INTE+) in health information communication has the potential to improve the care processes and decrease costs (ECCO+). Competitive advantage and profitability directly correlate with ease of integration and integration of legacy systems [AYA 07].

Consequently, we can suggest a relative correlation between these two factors. It could be a positive correlation between INTE+ and ECCO+ (the more reliable the ERP system's interoperability is, the more competitiveness would increase due to an ERP system: a positive arbitration of ROI). However, it could also be a positive correlation between INTE– and ECCO– (the more unreliable an ERP's interoperability is, the more competitiveness could not increase due to an ERP: a negative arbitration of ROI).

5.12. Correlation between ECCO and ESES

The amount of resources required depends on how well the ERP system fits with existing business processes:

– if business processes are closely aligned with the best practices model built into the ERP system, the need for extra resources will be minimized;

– if there is not a close match, a process of mutual adaptation is needed, in which the company may need to both adapt some of its business processes to align with those of the ERP system, and have the ERP system adapted to existing processes that cannot be changed [HON 02].

Firms have to adopt new architectures in response to new business strategies to cope with environment problems. In this way, they will probably be competitive [TRA 13].

Organizations develop IS strategies that interrelate with their business strategies and that together support corporate missions [ROG 94]. Therefore, the evolution strategy of existing systems (ESES) information technology (IT) is impacted by the business strategy of the firms. So, if the business strategy targets a reduction of costs, in this case it is better to adopt urbanization, because a total overhaul would be more expensive. "How to modernize without erasing the past, within the cost limits set, and do so while continuing to operate business while the work is carried out?" [LON 09]. The author explained that the principles of urbanization (ESES–) are to modernize and judiciously profit from technological advances within the cost limits set (ECCO+). Urbanization may be regarded as one of the keys to achieving competitive advantage through IT [TRA 13].

However, making a clean sweep (ESES+) of the existing IS on the basis of a new homogenous and modern solution does not seem to be the best solution functionally or economically (ECCO–) or humanly [LON 01]. Making a clean sweep is costly. Therefore, urbanization offers an evolution possibility that would be less expensive within the context of an economic crisis.

Consequently, we can suggest a relative correlation between these two factors. It could be a positive correlation between ESES– and ECCO+ (the more urbanization is performed, the more competitiveness would increase due to an ERP system: a positive arbitration of ROI). It could also be a positive correlation between ESES+ and ECCO– (the more total overhaul is performed, the more competitiveness could not increase due to an ERP: a negative arbitration of ROI). In other words, it could be a negative correlation between ESES+↗ and ECCO+↘ and the same between ESES–↗ and ECCO–↘.

5.13. Correlation between ECCO and COER

An ERP system must be simple and easy to understand for the average IT user, because ERP systems work efficiency influences the results of the organization [MON 96]. In order to maintain productivity, the software has to be simple to understand and easy to use after a reasonable amount of time spent getting acquainted with the system [ZET 04]. Competitive advantage and profitability correlate directly with ease of use, ease of operations and ease of learning. The simplicity of use of an ERP system determines the productivity of an organization [AYA 07]. Thus, in order to maximize work performance (ECCO+) and user satisfaction, the amount of complexity perceived by the user must be minimized (COER+).

The introduction of complex ERP systems has often shown to have negative unexpected side-effects such as decreased instead of increased order and control [HAN 06]. Eliminating difficult or obstructive interaction patterns on the user interface level is important. The usability of business software has become an important differentiator for success. Product training is often a reaction to front-end complexity (COER–), major changes in personal workflows and steep learning curves. Yet, it is an effective way to simplify the user's acquaintance with a new complex product and to increase productivity. However, end user training is costly (ECCO–) and only reasonable for central software products that are used frequently and continuously [UFL 07]. Thus, expensive training that could affect or decrease the competitiveness of firms (ECCO–) is necessary when the ERP system is complex (COER–).

Consequently, we can suggest a relative correlation between these two factors. It could be a positive correlation between COER+ and ECCO+ (the more simple an ERP system is, the more competitiveness would increase due to an ERP system). It could also be a positive correlation between COER– and ECCO– (the more complex an ERP system is, the more competitiveness could not increase due to an ERP). In other words, it could be a negative correlation between COER+↗ and ECCO–↘ and the same between COER–↗ and ECCO+↘.

5.14. Correlation between ECCO and ESEV

System upgrade is one of the main jobs of post-implementation and a system support phase [NAH 01]. It helps to extend the duration of the system's use as a long-term investment. ERP systems can provide the organization with a competitive advantage through improved business performance by integrating supply chain management, receiving, inventory management, and customer orders management, among other things [HIT 02, KAL 03]. A reliable ERP system's functionality helps to optimize business processes and lead to an increase in work efficiency [HAN 04]. Competitive advantage and profitability (ECCO+) correlate directly with functionality (ESEV+) and module completion [AYA 07].

ERP system functionality should be focused on the functional areas that are closest to generating profit, e.g. the supply chain, inventory or client relationships management. This functionality must work properly and efficiently with the goal to extend the system's functional capacity [RAT 12]. Firms are affected by decreases in their market share (ECCO–) because their ISs are not flexible enough to support new products, new services or customers' needs (ESEV–). As an alternative, firms have to adopt new architectures in response to new business strategies to cope with environment problems. In this way, they will probably be competitive [TRA 13]. Consequently, new subsystems or new modules (CRM, product lifecycle management (PLM), SCM, etc.) should be developed to provide these new functionalities.

Since the business environment is constantly changing, some necessary upgrades (from ERP 1st to 2nd G) need to be implemented during the whole ERP lifecycle, or the firm may not be able to remain competitive. The ERP system upgrade incurs costs which are approximately 25–33% of the initial investment [CAR 00]. The cost of each upgrade includes 50% of the original software license fee and 20% of the original implementation cost per user [SWA 04]. The cost of ERP system upgrades is high [MON 04]. Competitive advantage and profitability correlate directly with upgrade potential [AYA 07].

Generally, the significant costs of a future upgrade should not dissuade the client from purchasing an ERP package. It should also not negatively affect the competitiveness of an IS whose ERP system's upgrading is costly (the more expensive it is to upgrade, the less likely the ERP system is to be selected by clients to be a part of their IS).

Regarding the costs associated with an upgrade, we suggest the following classification:

1) upgrading to an ERP 2nd G that was developed by a vendor via an internal development is less expensive;

2) upgrading to an ERP 2nd G that was developed by a vendor via an external acquisition is more expensive. The introduction of new modules, especially after the acquisition of the vendor that made the software by a competitor, generates significant costs [DES 04];

3) upgrading an IS that is composed of an ERP 1st G that was kept by the vendor without any expansion toward a 2nd G or because that the vendor went out of business is very expensive.

Consequently, we can suggest a relative correlation between these two factors. It could be a positive correlation between ESEV+ and ECCO+ (the more an ERP 2nd G is developed in the first place by a vendor according to an internal development and then in the second place according to an external acquisition, the more the firm's competitiveness could increase due to this ERP system). It could also be a positive correlation between ESEV– and ECCO– (the more an ERP 1st G is kept without any expansion toward a 2nd G, the more the firm's competitiveness could not increase due to this ERP). In other words, it could be a negative correlation between ESEV+↗ and ECCO–↘ and the same between ESEV–↗ and ECCO+↘.

5.15. Correlation between TDEV and INTE

"According to the vendor SAP, its software package is highly modular (TDEV–) and components coexist harmoniously with other vendors (INTE+) such as Microsoft and Oracle" [NAU 08]. The ERP system modules were integrated one after another, but companies generally only incorporated between one and three [DES 04]. Therefore, ERP interoperability plays an important role within the IS and it should be improved.

As a result, we can suggest a relative correlation between these two factors. It could be a positive correlation between TDEV– and INTE+ (the more independent the firm is from the ERP system vendor, the more reliable the ERP system's interoperability should be). It could also be a positive correlation between TDEV+ and INTE– (the more dependent the firm is on the ERP vendor, the more unreliable the ERP system's interoperability could be. For example, the ERP system's interoperability is not important when the IS of the firm consists only of an ERP 2nd G). In other words, it could be a negative correlation between TDEV–↗ and INTE–↘ and the same between TDEV+↗ and INTE+↘.

5.16. Correlation between TDEV and ESES

One of the advantages of independence from an ERP system vendor (TDEV–) is the ability of firms to freely choose the evolution strategy of their existing systems: total overhaul or urbanization, which is widely preferred by firms. For example:

– if a firm prefers to complete its ERP 1st G by other subsystems such as IS number 5 as shown in Table 1.2, urbanization would be possible;

– it is not difficult for a firm whose architecture consists of only two modules of an ERP system with other subsystems to adopt a total overhaul or an urbanization strategy that leads to the replacement of its existing system or at least the replacement of its ERP system).

On the contrary, total dependence on the ERP system vendor (TDEV+) does not allow the firms to freely choose a given strategy. For example:

– if all modules of an ERP 2nd G are chosen by a firm to replace its existing system that is not an ERP 1st G, a total overhaul would be the only possible strategy to apply;

– if a firm asks its ERP system vendor for a migration from 1st to 2nd G, urbanization would be the only possible strategy to apply;

– it is very difficult for a firm, whose architecture consists mainly of many modules of an ERP system, to adopt a total overhaul because this evolution strategy leads to the replacement of its ERP system (virtually all IS needs to be replaced). In fact an urbanization that completes and improves its ERP system would be easier to achieve.

Consequently, we can suggest a relative correlation between these two factors. It could be a positive correlation between TDEV+↗ and ESES+ and – ↘ (the more independent the firm is from the ERP system vendor, the more freely the firm could choose its evolution strategy of existing systems). However, it could be a negative correlation between TDEV+↗ and ESES+ and − ↘ (the more totally dependent the firm is on the ERP system vendor, the less freely the firm could choose its evolution strategy of existing systems).

5.17. Correlation between PMER and INTE

Implementation and administration of additional functionality mostly requires special skills related to a specific system support (PMER+), because the biggest ERP vendors (SAP, Oracle and Microsoft) create solutions using their own platforms' technological linkages (INTE+) between hardware and software [AYA 07].

Consequently, we can suggest a relative correlation between these two factors. It could be a positive correlation between PMER+ and INTE+ (the more reliable the project management of an ERP system is, the more reliable the ERP system's interoperability with other subsystems could be; or *vice versa*, the more reliable an ERP system's interoperability is, the more reliable the project management of the ERP system could be). However, it could also be a positive correlation between PMER−↗ and INTE−↗ (the more unreliable the project management of an ERP system is, the more unreliable the ERP system's interoperability with other subsystems could be; or vice versa, the more unreliable the ERP system's interoperability is, the more unreliable the project management of the ERP system could be).

5.18. Correlation between PMER and ESES

An ERP system implementation project may cause a significant number of changes within an organization [DAV 00]. Several reasons prompted the 33.3% of firms that do not urbanize their IS. According to Trabelsi *et al.* [TRA 13], the main reason firms did not update their IS was the absence and unavailability of skilled labor (16.6%) or the lack of high and specific qualification (PMER−) crucial for urbanization (ESES−). In fact, within the framework of an ERP system's project management, a high level of skills is crucial regardless of the evolution strategy of the existing system (urbanization or total overhaul: ESES − or +).

Therefore, we can suggest a relative correlation between these two factors. It could be a negative correlation between PMER– and ESES– or + (the more unreliable the project management of an ERP system is, the less likely urbanization or total overhaul could be performed with success). However, it could be a positive correlation between PMER+ and ESES– or + (the more reliable the project management of an ERP system is, the more likely urbanization or total overhaul could be performed with success).

5.19. Correlation between PMER and COER

ERP system implementation is a complex process, and there have been many cases of unsuccessful implementation [PAR 00]. Complexity of implementation is a measure of the internal effort with respect to the time and effort involved in the configuration, documentation, training and support functions of the ERP system implementation [LAL 06].

Training users to use an ERP system is essential because it is not easy to use even with good computer skills (ZHA 02, NAH 03, WOO 07]. ERP systems are extremely complex and demand rigorous training. Wei *et al.* [WEI 05] define the simplicity of an ERP system using ease of use (COER+) as a measure for the simplicity of training and use (PMER+). The less complex an ERP system is, the more successful project management can be, because training will be easier. Selection of a complex ERP system leads to complex project management.

Consequently, we can suggest a relative correlation between these two factors. It could be a positive correlation between COER+ and PMER+ (the more simple an ERP system is, the more reliable the project management of an ERP system could be). It could also be a positive correlation between COER– and PMER– (the more complex an ERP system is, the more unreliable the project management of an ERP system could be). However, it could be a negative correlation between COER+↗ and PMER–↘ (the more simple an ERP system is, the less unreliable the project management of an ERP system could be) and the same between COER–↗ and PMER+↘ (the more complex an ERP system is, the less reliable its project management could be).

5.20. Correlation between PMER and ESEV

A sophisticated definition of ERP vendor reputation has been introduced by Verveille and Hallinten [VER 03], which highlights vendor recognition, technological and strategical vision, longevity and experience performing implementation projects. According to Ayağ and Özdemir [AYA 07], implementation and administration of additional functionality (ESEV+) mostly requires special skills (PMER+). In order to successfully manage the whole upgrade process (ESEV+ and −), appropriate implementation and planning methodologies (PMER+) should be used to define changes in the organizational structure [RAT 12].

No matter what generation an ERP system is (1st or 2nd), the project management should be reliable. However, we remember that an external acquisition strategy does not allow a vendor to develop its ERP 2nd G on the founding principles of a total integration "TIIS" (see section 4.7). As a result, the project management should be more organized, sophisticated and difficult for an ERP 2nd G developed by a vendor according to an external acquisition compared to an ERP 2nd G developed according to an internal development.

Consequently, we can suggest a relative correlation between these two factors. It could be a positive correlation between ESEV+ and PMER+ (the more an ERP 2nd G is developed in the first place by a vendor according to an external acquisition and then in the second place according to an internal development, the more reliable the project management to implement this ERP system should be). It could also be a positive correlation between ESEV− and PMER+ (the more an ERP 1st G is kept without any expansion toward a 2nd G, the more reliable the project management to integrate this ERP system with other subsystems should be). However, it could be a negative relationship between ESEV+↗ and PMER−↘ and the same between ESEV−↗ and PMER−↘.

5.21. Correlation between INTE and ESES

To evaluate ERP software suitability, we have to consider its integration possibilities with software already in use [SPR 00, EVE 00, KUM 02, KUM 03, VER 03, FIS 04, BUE 08, RAT 12]. "One ERP cannot meet all users' needs and a company may wish to keep an existing specific application. The ERP must coexist with other applications. When the existing system is highly specific and the ERPs cannot meet a part of the business needs, interoperability is crucial" [MAR 01].

Technically, an urbanized IS is interoperable in a manner that demonstrates the faculty for two heterogeneous computer systems to function jointly and to give access to their resources in a reciprocal way [CHE 08a]. The model of system development has changed since the mid-1990s, with a move toward so-called urbanization (ESES–), where systems are constructed from existing components and applications and where new systems have to integrate and interoperate (INTE+) with a range of existing systems [HOP 08]. We address the importance of urbanization to ensure interoperability. The result showed a strong relationship between these two variables. There is statistically significant correlation between urbanization (ESES-) and interoperability (INTE+). That is, increases or decreases in urbanization do significantly relate to increases or decreases in the interoperability of IS. The result confirms that urbanization leads to IS interoperability [TRA 13].

When the existing system is specific or extremely complex and the ERP system's interoperability is unreliable (INTE–), urbanization (ESES–) to interface this ERP system with the existing system becomes very difficult to achieve. In this case, a total overhaul (ESES+), of this specific or extremely complex existing, would maybe be the only option. However, a total overhaul, which aims to implement an ERP system with some extremely complex software, could also be difficult to accomplish when the ERP system's interoperability is unreliable (in this case, a reliable interoperability "INTE+" would be crucial). Thus, a relationship could be suggested between ESES– or + and INTE– (unreliable interoperability is not suitable for urbanization or total overhaul). Nevertheless, some exceptions could make this relationship less important. For example, when a total overhaul is adopted to implement an ERP 2nd G, which will be the only component of the IS, ERP system interoperability is not important.

Therefore, we can suggest a relative correlation between these two factors. It could be a positive correlation between INTE+ and ESES– or + (the more reliable an ERP system's interoperability is, the more urbanization or total overhaul could be performed with success). However, it could be a negative relationship between INTE–↗ and ESES– or +↘ (the more unreliable an ERP system's interoperability is, the less urbanization or total overhaul could be performed with success).

5.22. Correlation between INTE and COER

With an increase in process integrity and automation, the level of functional interdependency between system modules increases, contributing to system complexity [UFL 07]. Most ERP packages are very complex (COER–), so interfacing with these systems is not an easy task (INTE–) [LEO 07, RAT 12].

Consequently, we can suggest a relative kind of correlation between these two factors. It could be a positive correlation between COER– and INTE– (the more complex an ERP system is, the more unreliable interoperability with this ERP system could be). For example, a complex ERP 1st G would be difficult to be interfaced and then to communicate with other applications within the IS. It could also be a positive relationship between COER+ and INTE+ (the more simple an ERP system is, the more reliable interoperability with this ERP system could be). For example, a simple ERP 2nd G that does not contain all possible modules could be easily interfaced with part of the legacy systems and it could communicate within the IS with them without many difficulties.

However, it could be a negative relationship between COER–↗ and INTE+↘ (the more complex an ERP system is, the less reliable interoperability with this ERP system could be) and also a negative relationship between COER+↗ and INTE–↘ (the more simple an ERP system is, the less unreliable interoperability with this ERP system could be).

5.23. Correlation between INTE and ESEV

"To best meet business needs, companies may integrate other specialized software products with the ERP. Interfaces for commercial software applications or legacy systems may need to be developed in-house if they are not available in the market" [BIN 99]. This citation from 1999 lets us suppose that the functionalities (modules) of ERP 1st G were incomplete and that the interoperability of ERP systems was not reliable due to the lack of necessary competency. Most firms will have some system that will not fit into the functionality of ERP packages and which will have to be interfaced with the ERP [LEO 07]. Exchanges with internal and external partners, suppliers and customers require the company to implement an interoperable IS [TRA 13].

A given evolution strategy of ERP system vendors (due to incomplete functionalities of an ERP system or lack of functional match, such as incapability of the ERP system to meet the business requirements of the firm) is closely related to its interoperability. For example, if the evolution strategy of an ERP system vendor does not aim to develop a complete functional perimeter (all necessary modules to meet the business needs of the firm), the ERP system's interoperability should be improved, especially when the IS of the firm consists of an ERP system with other subsystems.

Therefore, we can suggest a relative correlation between these two factors. It could be a positive correlation between ESEV− and INTE+ (the more an ERP 1st G is kept without any expansion toward a 2nd G, the more reliable the ERP's interoperability should be). It is also a positive correlation between ESEV+ and INTE+ (the more an ERP 2nd G is developed by a vendor according to an internal development or to an external acquisition, the more reliable an ERP system's interoperability should be). In fact, often even when an ERP 2nd G is selected, firms do not purchase all of the available modules and thus their ISs are generally completed and interfaced with other subsystems. However, the interoperability would only be rarely important when the IS of a firm consists only of an ERP 2nd G that was developed by a vendor according to an internal development, without any another subsystem.

However, it could be a negative correlation between ESEV−↗ and INTE−↘ (the more an ERP 1st G is kept without any expansion toward a 2nd G, the less unreliable the interoperability of this ERP system could be); and it could also be a negative correlation between ESEV+↗ and INTE−↘ (the more an ERP 2nd G is developed by a vendor according to an internal development or to an external acquisition, the less unreliable the interoperability of this ERP system could be).

5.24. Correlation between COER and ESEV

Generally, the ERPs 1st G were rather complex packages. For example, the following indicators demonstrate the complexity of SAP R/3: this ERP solution currently includes 20 industry-specific solutions, more than 200 finer grained business objects, 400 business application interfaces (BAPIs) and more than 800 reference process models [CUR 98]. The SAP reference data model contains more than 4,000 entity types (see for [ROD 98]). When considering the possible upgrades of the current ERP (ESEV), several issues are important: how easy the transition to the newest version (COER) is and what kind of modifications the systems' vendors are planning to launch during the next 3–5 years [HEC 97]. When the ERP package is complex, upgrading it would not be easy to accomplish within the IS.

As a result, we can suggest a relative correlation between these two factors. It could be a positive correlation between COER+ and ESEV+ (the simpler an ERP system is, the easier an evolution strategy of ERP vendors toward an ERP 2nd G by an internal development or by an external acquisition is, and thus it would be easier for clients to upgrade). However, it could be a negative correlation between COER–↗ and ESEV+↘ (the more complex an ERP system is, the less easy an evolution strategy of ERP vendors toward an ERP 2nd G by an internal development or by an external acquisition is, and the less updating for clients is simple).

However, it is possible to better detail this correlation between COER+ and ESEV+. As we have found above in the literature review, it seems that evolving to an ERP 2nd G by an internal development is easier for vendors to achieve compared to evolving to an ERP 2nd G accomplished by an external acquisition. This observation allows us to distinguish inside the variable "ESEV+" between two different levels of upgrading driven by firms:

– the first one is an upgrade to an ERP 2nd G that is achieved by the vendor according to an internal development;

– the second one is an upgrade to an ERP 2nd G developed by the vendor according to an external acquisition.

According to this distinction, it is possible to suggest that the first upgrade strategy could be simpler for clients than the second upgrade strategy. In other words, the more an ERP 2nd G is developed in the first place by a vendor according to an internal development and then in the second place according to an external acquisition, the simpler this ERP system could be, and thus updating would be easier for clients.

It could also be a positive correlation between COER– and ESEV– (the more complex an ERP 1st G is, the more likely an evolution strategy of ERP vendors could be to keep this ERP system without any expansion toward a 2nd G or by the vendor going out of business, and thus the more complex it could be for clients to upgrade this ERP 1st G within the IS). However, it could be a negative correlation between COER+↗ and ESEV–↘ (the simpler an ERP 1st G is, the less evolution strategy of ERP vendors could consist of keeping this ERP without any expansion toward a 2nd G or by the vendor going out of business, and thus the less complex upgrading this ERP 1st G within the IS could be).

According to an exploration of the literature and logical deduction, we can assume that correlations between our chosen research factors have been established. Generally, the suggested correlations between the research factors could be summarized as illustrated in Table 5.1.

	Correlation between the research factors	ECCO		TDEV		PMER		INTE		ESES		COER		ESEV	
		+	-	+	-	+	-	+	-	+	-	+	-	+	-
ECCO	+ Competitiveness would be improved thanks to an ERP (a positive arbitration of ROI)					PC									
	- Competitiveness could not be improved thanks to an ERP (a negative arbitration of ROI)				PC										
TDEV	+ Total dependency on the ERP vendor														
	- Independence from the ERP vendor														
PMER	+ Reliable ERP project management	PC													
	- Unreliable ERP project management		PC												
INTE	+ Reliable interoperability of the ERP	PC				NC	PC	PC							
	- Unreliable interoperability of the ERP		PC			PC	NC		PC						
ESES	+ Total overhaul performed, especially, on extremely complex existing	NC	PC	NC	PC	PC	NC	PC	NC						
	- Urbanization performed on a simple or a complex existing	PC	NC	NC	PC	PC	NC	PC	NC						
COER	+ Simple ERP	PC	NC					PC	NC	PC	NC				
	- Complex ERP	NC	PC					NC	PC	NC	PC				
ESEV	+ Evolution to an ERP 2nd G by an internal development or by an external acquisition	PC	NC					PC	NC	PC	NC	PC	NC		
	- keeping an ERP 1st G without any expansion towards a 2nd G or by the vendor going out of business	NC	PC					PC	NC	PC	NC	NC	PC		

Table 5.1. *Correlations between research factors. Positive correlation (PC) negative correlation (NC)*

6

Case Studies

In this chapter, three case studies have been conducted: the first two case studies analyze the information systems (IS) of Hershey and FoxMeyer Drugs, both of which have already implemented enterprise resource planning (ERP) systems; while the third case study studies the strategy of Oracle as a software vendor. We briefly describe the IS evolution for each firm with an analysis of the impact of the research factors on relationships between ERP systems and IS integration or disintegration.

6.1. Hershey

Hershey, which was founded in 1894, sold several products: Kisses, Kit Kat, Reeses peanut butter cups, Twizzlers, etc. In 1996, Hershey chose to replace its legacy systems. There was growing demand from its retailers for suppliers such as Hershey to share their product delivery data so that the retailers could maintain optimum inventory levels and reduce costs.

Hershey selected SAP R/3, along with companion software from two vendors: Manugistics (supply chain software) and Siebel (customer relationship management (CRM)) = "*TDEV–*". Software from systems, applications and products for data processing (SAP) included modules for finance, purchasing, materials management, warehousing, order processing and billing. Manugistics provided software for transport management, production, forecasting and scheduling. Siebel was to support Hershey in managing customer relations and in tracking the effectiveness of the company's marketing through a pricing promotions module. Hershey had used software from Manugistics earlier in its mainframes = "evolution strategy of existing systems *(ESES–)*".

At this period, even if Hershey would have preferred purchasing SAP's supply chain management (SCM) and CRM modules over those of Manugistics and Siebel, it would not have been possible, because SAP did not offer these modules to clients in 1996. In fact, before 2002, the vendors' strategies (SAP, Oracle, etc.) did not take into consideration the new modules that seem vital today (CRM, SCM, etc.). At that time, these modules were commercialized by certain Best of Breed companies such as Siebel and Manugistics. SAP was keeping its ERP 1st G without any expansion toward a 2nd G, and we therefore define the evolution strategy of this ERP vendor *(ESEV)* information technology (IT).

IBM Global Services was chosen as the integrator. Accenture and SAP helped the IT teams to complete implementation. In order to speed up the project (30 months instead of 4 years), Hershey then decided on a Big Bang approach, where several modules were implemented simultaneously, instead of a phased approach designed to find and correct bugs before moving on to the next phase. The employees needed to be trained on the system functionality and also on how the different modules interacted with each other. They were overloaded, as they had to learn the intricacies of not one, but three new systems, and bring out the required revisions in their activities = *"PMER–"*.

Hershey's former CEO and Chairman Kenneth L. Wolfe told Wall Street analysts during a conference call at the end of 1999 that the company was having problems with its new order-taking and distribution system. Slowly, problems pertaining to order fulfillment processing and shipping started to arise. Several consignments were shipped behind schedule, and even among those, several deliveries were incomplete. Customers began switching to products of competitors such as Nestlé and Mars. Moreover, orders from many retailers and distributors could not be fulfilled, even though Hershey had the finished product stocked in its warehouses. The company said that the new systems were not transmitting order details to the warehouses and the data flow between different applications needed to be corrected in order to fix the problems = *"INTE–"*.

"The reduction in shipments resulted primarily from difficulties in order fulfillment (customer service, warehousing, and shipping) encountered since the start-up of a new integrated information system (IIS) and new business processes during the third quarter of 1999" (Hershey, annual report 1999). The results of failed ERP system implementations were immediate, with a significant drop in the revenues for third quarter of 1999. Annual revenues for 1999 were US$150 million less compared to those in 1998, a drop of 12% = "*ECCO–*".

Experts and analysts were of the view that:

– with three different vendors working on the system, it would have been better if Hershey had chosen to roll out each system successively and then check the integration issues ="INTE–". "There were three cooks in that kitchen. That's why there is so much finger-pointing going on" [OST 00];

– problems could have been avoided if there had been more focus on training = "PMER–";

– "these systems tie together in very intricate ways, and things that work fine in testing can turn out to be a disaster" (Shepard, Vice president for AMR research 1999). Aside from the fact that SAP itself was complex to install and run, Hershey attempted to implement two other applications along with it, making the whole exercise still more complex = "*COER–*";

– with more than one package in operation, there was a sharp increase in the number of touch points and interfaces, and implementation-related problems were almost inevitable. There were problems integrating SAP with Siebel and Manugistics ="*INTE–*".

The upgrade of the failed project began in July 2001 and was finished in May 2002. Hershey redesigned the process and began working with SAP 4.6. According to Joe Zakutney, Director, SAP at Hershey, "the company's success in its second round of ERP implementation was attributable to strong program management and executive leadership diligent planning and an extensive testing and training plan [WEI 02]"= "*PMER+*". Within 11 months, the system was implemented successfully.

The lack of interoperability within the framework of the IS was one of the primary reasons for the original project's failure. In order to address this issue, Hershey improved the interface between distribution function and SAP = "*INTE+*". Hershey said it was able to make more than 30 improvements to its core business processes. The company cited enhancements such as the automation of pick-list processing and materials management invoice verification, plus credit processing for distributors to military customers. These improvements have helped reduce costs = "*ECCO+*" and speed up processing times.

6.1.1. *Case outcome and evaluation*

Hershey is an interesting case study for our research, because, after a first round of an unsuccessful ERP system implementation (a kind of IS disintegration), a second round enabled Hershey to achieve a successful ERP system implementation (integration).

Before the successful updating in 2001, the integration problems between the three subsystems (SAP, Siebel and Manugistics) were related to the unreliability of the interoperability and to the ERP system's complexity. Therefore, "INTE–" and "COER–" have been given as values. In fact, prior to 2000, before the successful update, the interoperability was not sufficiently developed by the ERP system vendors and to this day, they are still working to improve it. Regarding the complexity, we consider that there is still much progress to be made by the ERP system vendors. However, after many years of usage and experience, SAP, Siebel and Manugistics became less complex for Hershey's employees.

Although improvements have been made, even after the successful updating in 2001, we cannot give the two factors "INTE and COER" positive values. In fact, we know that in September 2005, Oracle Corporation acquired Siebel. As we explained previously (see factor ESEV), the redesigning of Siebel into Oracle could be performed only in a more or less integrated way, which is complex enough. Therefore, the interfacing of Oracle with the rest of the architecture (mainly SAP) is not easy to implement. This is why we give values between "– and +" for INTE and COER.

Regarding the evolution strategy of ERP vendors, we already said that in September 2005, Oracle Corporation acquired Siebel, which thus went out of business = "ESEV–". However, by instituting an external acquisition, Oracle allows us also to give this factor the value of "ESEV+". Hershey's update into new versions, with all of its subsystems within a large vision, became even more difficult because of the expansion strategies of their ERP system vendors. As a result, we also give values between "– and +" for ESEV.

All of the research factors that have been discussed and detected by the literature review have been confirmed by the Hershey case study. Although the firm's aim was to implement an IIS, this case study illustrated two types of IS evolution (first a disintegration and then an integration):

– the first round of this project management (before 2000), which was a failure, did not allow this goal to be reached. The negative values, which have been detected for all factors, have led to a disintegrated information system (DIS) instead of the desired IIS. We can conclude that the combination of negative values of all factors caused the ERP system's evolution to promote IS disintegration;

– the second round of the project (after 2001), which was a success, allowed the architecture to transform from a DIS to an hybrid integration of IS (HIIS). The values of certain factors have changed (economic crisis and competitiveness (ECCO), project management ERP (PMER), complexity of ERP (COER), interoperability of the ERP (INTE) and ESEV)), while other values have not changed (total dependency on the ERP vendor (TDEV) and ESES). We can conclude that the new combination of values favors an HIIS.

6.2. FoxMeyer Drugs

FoxMeyer Drugs was a $5 billion company and the fourth largest distributor of pharmaceuticals in the United States before the fiasco. With the goal of using technology to increase efficiency, the Delta III project began in 1993. FoxMeyer purchased SAP in December 1993, as well as warehouse-automation from a vendor called Pinnacle = "*TDEV–*" and chose Andersen Consulting to integrate and implement the two systems. Implementation of the project took place during 1994 and 1995. The firm was driven to bankruptcy in 1996 = "*ECCO–*", and the trustee of FoxMeyer announced in 1998 that he was suing SAP as well as Andersen Consulting for $500 million each [CAL 98]. The reasons for the failure were the following:

– the processes of the business practices were not reengineered to be adapted to fit the new design integration (SAP and Pinnacle). Some users were not fully committed since the project threatened their jobs. This meant resistance to change and rejection of the tool by users. In addition, a shortage of skilled and knowledgeable personnel was crucial. There were over 50 consultants at FoxMeyer, many inexperienced, and the turnover was high. According to FoxMeyer, Andersen used the project as a training ground for "consultants who were very inexperienced" [COM 98]. Besides, despite warnings from Woltz Consulting during the early stages of the project that an 18-month schedule for the entire implementation to be completed was unrealistic = "*PMER–*", Delta project went ahead [JES 97];

– the decision to go with two different vendors = "*TDEV–*" for two of the company's most important business systems was "an error in information processing" [KEI 95]. This added still greater complexity to an already challenging situation [JES 97], given the integration's original complexity (SAP and Pinnacle subsystems). The warehouse automation multiplied the project risk, and interactions between SAP and Pinnacle's automation took FoxMeyer into uncharted waters = "*INTE–*". Using just one vendor in the first phase would have reduced the risks and complexity of the project = "*COER–*".

6.2.1. *Case outcome and evaluation*

We think that the subsystem of warehouse-automation was not bought from SAP for one of the two reasons:

– this module was not taken into account within the evolution strategy of SAP in 1994;

– FoxMeyer did not want to be dependent on one ERP vendor.

This is why we gave both factors the negative values = "ESEV– and TDEV–".

6.3. Oracle Corporation's E-Business Suite

This case study is prepared from many interviews that were retrieved from the Internet of certain directors of Oracle: Larry Ellison, a co-founder of Oracle Corporation and Jimmy Anidjar, who was Senior Vice President Oracle France and MEA (Middle East and Africa). Some responses of these interviews are given in the study. Therefore, this case study represents the vendor's point of view combined with our analysis.

Oracle is a multinational computer technology corporation based in the United States that specializes in developing and marketing computer hardware systems, databases and ERP systems. "In 2004, we bought

PeopleSoft. We had three ERPs, two CRMs, two HR systems and it became even more complicated with the arrival of Siebel. Since the beginning of 2005, Oracle has made no less than 27 acquisitions. The latest is that of Hyperion in 2007 which was a Best of Breed in Business Intelligence (BI). We knew we had to create a new generation of ERP, assembling the best features of PeopleSoft, JD Edwards, Oracle E-Business Suite, Siebel, decision making and advanced collaborative tools = "*ESEV+*". Our goal is to help customers replace application silos by an ERP wide scope announced in Q1 2011" [ELL 10]. Oracle sought to standardize its offerings and build a growing number of products on the same foundation.

"It took five years and a lot of work to get there. The Suite contains 10,000 unique integrated processes and the final version will include 100 different products. We had never done this before, and I hope we will not have to do it again = "*COER–*"" [ELL 10]. "How then can one design a new ERP based on many ERPs (different technologies and formats)? After heavy rewriting and production of a new version of the ERP which takes into account, in a more or less integrated way, the modules recently acquired, we obtain a wider perimeter of the ERP. But for firms, updated versions become very cumbersome as the new redesigned ERP is technically quite different from the previous and such a scenario could happen again in the future" [PRA 08].

Oracle also seeks to promote the interoperability of the final version, which contains an application integration architecture that includes middleware interoperability. This orchestration allows the linking of functions either from the existing software package or other solutions that may or may not be Oracle software. "We know that the introduction of new modules, especially after the acquisition of the vendor that made the software, by a competitor generates a lot of difficulties without guaranteed result" [DES 04]. Even though the interoperability's improvement was taken into account by Oracle, we cannot know if this interoperability was completely reliable. For this reason, we choose to give values between "*– and +*" *for INTE.*

Oracle's clients can decide whether to purchase the whole package or only some modules = "TDEV–", but whatever the migration tools provided by Oracle, we can expect that migration is an important project = "PMER+", as the ERP is built on a new foundation. New customers are oriented to this new coherent offer (if new clients would like to buy the whole package, a total overhaul will be necessary to replace their existing systems = "ESES+"). Old customers can keep old products, which continue to evolve (if old clients would like to buy only a part of the package, an urbanization would be sufficient = "ESES–"). We note that the factor ESES adopted by firms is taken into account by the vendor.

6.3.1. *Case outcome and evaluation*

This case study permits an analysis of the evolution strategy of an ERP system vendor. We think that the implementation of Oracle, which represents an ERP 2nd G developed by the vendor according to a strategy of external acquisition, promotes an HIIS rather than a total integration of IS (TIIS) (see Table 1.1).

6.4. Summary of case studies

Contrary to a simple software or subsystem, a complicated ERP system needs a considerable amount of training. The tests, especially integration tests, have not been carried out correctly. Therefore, a "PMER–" has generated an "INTE–". It seems, in the late 1990s and early 2000s, the enlargement of the ERP perimeter was limited to an ERP 1st G without any new modules such as CRM, SCM, BI, etc. As a result, the only possible value, at this time, for the ESEV is "–". Contrary to the main goal for the two firms that targeted an IIS implementation, some combinations of factor values have led to a kind of IS disintegration. Other combinations for Hershey after their successful upgrade have allowed a kind of integration by an evolution from a DIS to an HIIS.

The case studies generally confirm the reliability of research factors explored previously, as well as the suggested correlations between these factors. These case studies also allow us to observe relationships between the research factors and IS integration or disintegration. According to a given combination of the mentioned factors' values, different architectures are observed (especially DIS and HIIS). Table 6.1 resumes the principal ideas of these three cases.

	TDEV	ECCO	COER	ESES	ESEV	PMER	INTE	IS
Hershey before success	−	−	−	−	−	−	−	*DIS*
Hershey after success	−	+	Between − and +	−	Between − and +	+	Between − and +	*HIIS*
FoxMeyer	−	−	−	NA	−	−	−	*DIS*
Oracle Corporation	−	NA	−	Between − and +	+	+	Between − and +	*HIIS*

Table 6.1. *Factors affecting the relationships between the evolution of ERP systems and IS integration or disintegration according to the case studies*

7

Discussion: Relationships between Evolution of ERP Systems and IS Integration or Disintegration

In this chapter, we discuss the meaning of the relationships between the research factors, evolution of enterprise resource planning (ERP) systems and information system (IS) integration or disintegration. Our analysis, interpretation, deduction and results are based on the case studies and the literature review. Depending on the combinations of the research factors, the impact of the evolution of ERP systems on IS integration or disintegration could be as follows.

7.1. TDEV and ECCO

Although ERP systems (by virtue of process integration) should logically help to improve the competitiveness of firms, an expensive total cost of ownership (TCO) of these packages could considerably reduce this competitiveness. As a result, the positive correlation between total dependency on the ERP vendor– (TDEV–) and economic crisis and competitiveness+ (ECCO+) (the more independent the firm is from an ERP system vendor, the more the firm's competitiveness would increase due to an ERP system: a positive arbitration of ROI) could not help to implement a total integration of IS (TIIS) (when a TCO of an ERP system is very expensive, the return on investment (ROI) could be positive in cases where the firm is not obliged to buy or keep the whole package and can choose only some modules due to the possibility of independence from one vendor. As a result, the IS would consist of more than one ERP system).

However, the identified positive correlation between TDEV+ and ECCO– (the more dependent the firm is on an ERP vendor, the more the firm's competitiveness could not increase due to an ERP system: a negative arbitration of ROI) could also fail to lead to a TIIS. (When a TCO of an ERP system is very expensive, the ROI could be negative in cases where the firm is obliged to buy or keep the whole package and cannot choose only some modules because of the obligation of dependence on their one vendor. As a result, the firm avoids buying or keeping the whole package, and thus the IS then would not consist of only one ERP system). However, we think that total dependency on the ERP system vendor could improve the firm's competitiveness provided that the TCO is inexpensive in a manner that could improve the ROI's arbitration. In this case, a firm could buy or keep the whole package, and thus, a TIIS could result.

7.2. TDEV and INTE

The positive correlation between TDEV– and interoperability of the ERP+ (INTE+) (the more independent the firm is from the ERP system vendor, the more reliable the interoperability of the ERP system should be) could help to implement an hybrid integration of IS (HIIS) according to Table 1.1 (with different vendors, the architecture would consist of many subsystems whose reliable interconnections could lead to a hybrid integration). The identified positive correlation between TDEV+ and INTE– (the more dependent the firm is on the ERP system vendor, the more unreliable the interoperability of the ERP system could be) could contribute to a TIIS according to Table 1.1 (with only one vendor, the whole architecture would consist of one ERP system, which does not need to be integrated with any other subsystem. For example, the interoperability of an ERP 2nd G becomes unimportant when the architecture is composed only of this one ERP system).

The explored negative correlation between TDEV– and INTE– (the more independent the firm is from the ERP system vendor, the less unreliable the interoperability of the ERP system could be) could encourage a kind of disintegration and lead to a disintegrated information system (DIS), especially when the unreliability of the ERP system's interoperability is important (with different vendors, the architecture would consist of many subsystems whose unreliable interconnections could provoke IS disintegration).

7.3. PMER and ESES

The positive correlation between project management ERP+ (PMER+) and evolution strategy of existing systems – or + (ESES– or +) (the more reliable the project management of the ERP system is, the more urbanization or total overhaul could be performed with success) could improve integration. For example, a TIIS could result if reliable project management of the ERP system, within the framework of a total overhaul or urbanization, leads to an ERP 2nd G developed by an ERP system vendor according to an internal development; or an HIIS could result if reliable project management of the ERP system, within the framework of urbanization, leads to an ERP 1st G that interfaces well with other subsystems within the whole IS.

On the contrary, the negative correlation between PMER– and ESES– or + (the more unreliable the project management of the ERP system is, the less urbanization or total overhaul could be performed with success) could lead to a kind of disintegration: e.g. a DIS could result if unreliable project management of the ERP system, within the framework of urbanization, leads to an ERP 1st G that is not well interfaced with other subsystems within the whole IS.

7.4. COER and PMER

The positive correlation between complexity of ERP+ (COER+) and PMER+ (the simpler the ERP system is, the more reliable the project management of the ERP system could be) could improve IS integration: e.g. a TIIS or an HIIS could be deployed if reliable project management is utilized to implement a simple ERP 2nd G developed by an ERP system vendor according to an internal development or an external acquisition. The positive correlation between COER– and PMER– (the more complex the ERP system is, the more unreliable the project management of the ERP system could be) could generally lead to a kind of disintegration: e.g. a DIS could result if unreliable project management is utilized to implement a complex ERP system that cannot be integrated with other subsystems easily.

The negative correlation between COER– and PMER+ (the more complex the ERP system is, the less reliable project management could be) could lead to integration as well as to disintegration: e.g. an HIIS could result if the reliability of the project management could offset the complexity of the ERP system; or maybe a DIS would result if the complexity of the

ERP system could not be offset by the reliability of the project management. The negative correlation between COER+ and PMER– (the simpler the ERP system is, the less unreliable project management could be) could also lead to integration as well as to disintegration: e.g. an HIIS could result if the simplicity of the ERP system could offset the unreliability of the project management; or a DIS would result if the simplicity of the ERP system could not offset the unreliability of the project management.

7.5. INTE and ESES

The positive correlation between INTE+ and ESES– or + (the more reliable the interoperability of the ERP system is, the more urbanization or total overhaul could be performed with success) could improve integration: e.g. an HIIS could result if the reliable interoperability of a selected ERP 1st G allows for good integration with other subsystems within the framework of urbanization or a total overhaul.

The negative correlation between INTE– and ESES– or + (the more unreliable the interoperability of the ERP system is, the less urbanization or total overhaul could be performed with success) could lead to a kind of disintegration: e.g. a DIS would result if the unreliable interoperability of a selected ERP 1st G does not allow for good integration with other subsystems within the framework of urbanization or a total overhaul.

7.6. COER and INTE

The combination between COER and INTE could also affect IS integration or disintegration. The positive relationship between COER+ and INTE+ (the simpler the ERP system is, the more reliable the interoperability with this ERP system could be) could improve IS integration: e.g. an HIIS could result if the simplicity of an ERP 1st G helps to establish reliable interoperability with the other subsystems within the whole IS.

On the contrary, the positive correlation between COER– and INTE– (the more complex the ERP system is, the more unreliable the interoperability with this ERP system could be) could lead to a kind of IS disintegration: e.g. a DIS could result if the complexity of an ERP 1st G leads to unreliable interoperability with other subsystems within the whole IS.

7.7. ESEV and INTE

The combination between evolution strategy of ERP vendors (ESEV) and INTE could affect IS integration or disintegration. The positive correlation between ESEV– or + and INTE+ (the more an ERP 1st G is kept without any expansion toward a 2nd G or the more an ERP 2nd G is developed by a vendor according to an internal development or an external acquisition, the more reliable the interoperability of the ERP system should be) could improve IS integration. Consequently, regardless of the expansion strategy of vendors (ESEV – or +), the interoperability of the ERP (1st or 2nd G) should be reliable. In fact, even the interoperability of an ERP 2nd G must be reliable, especially in cases where all modules are not selected by the client. The reliable interoperability allows for the integration of certain modules (ERP 2nd G) within the framework of the whole IS.

Examples:

– An HIIS could be obtained if the evolution strategy of the ERP vendor (ESEV–) aims to improve the ERP system's interoperability in a manner that easily allows for good integration between an ERP 1st G and the rest of the IS.

– An HIIS could also be obtained if the evolution strategy of the ERP vendor (ESEV+) aims to improve the ERP system's interoperability in a manner that easily allows for good communication between some modules of an ERP 2nd G and some legacy systems.

On the contrary, the negative correlation between ESEV– or + and INTE– (the more an ERP 1st G is kept without any expansion toward a 2nd G or the more an ERP 2nd G is developed by a vendor according to an internal development or an external acquisition, the less unreliable the interoperability of this ERP system could be) could lead to a kind of IS disintegration. In fact, if the ERP system's interoperability is not reliable, the IS integration would be compromised and a kind of disintegration could affect the whole architecture.

Examples:

– A DIS could result if the evolution strategy of the ERP vendor (ESEV–) does not aim to improve the ERP system's interoperability in a manner that does not allow for the establishment of an integration between an ERP 1st G with other subsystems within the whole IS.

– A DIS could also result if the interoperability of an ERP 2nd G that is developed by a vendor according to an external acquisition (ESEV+) is unreliable in a manner that does not permit good communication between the different modules within this ERP 2nd G or between some modules of this ERP 2nd G and some legacy systems.

Nevertheless, the relationship between ESEV+ and INTE– could, in one special case, lead to a kind of total IS integration. For example, a TIIS could be achieved when an ERP 2nd G that is developed by an ERP system vendor according to an internal development is implemented as the only component of the whole IS. In this special case, the ERP system's interoperability is not important.

7.8. COER and ESEV

The positive correlation between COER+ and ESEV+ (the simpler the ERP system is, the easier an evolution strategy of ERP vendors toward an ERP 2nd G by an internal development or an external acquisition is, and thus the simpler it is for clients to update the system) could improve IS integration.

Examples:

– A TIIS could be obtained if a simple ERP 2nd G that is developed by a vendor according to an internal development is implemented as the only component of the whole IS.

– An HIIS could be obtained if a simple ERP 2nd G that is developed by a vendor according to an external acquisition is implemented as a part of the whole IS, which becomes easy to use by employees.

On the contrary, the negative correlation between COER– and ESEV+ (the more complex an ERP system is, the less easy an evolution strategy of ERP vendors toward an ERP 2nd G by an internal development or an external acquisition is, and thus the less simple it is for clients to update the system) could lead to a kind of IS disintegration: e.g. a DIS could result if some modules of a complex ERP 2nd G that is developed by a vendor according to an external acquisition are implemented as a part of the whole IS, which becomes very difficult to manage by users.

As we notice from our analysis (including the correlations between research factors, case studies and discussion), the correlation is not only binary between a couple of factors. In fact, each factor is, more or less, correlated to other factors. Therefore, most of these factors are intercorrelated. Generally, we can propose a typology that underlines the role of the combination of research factors affecting the relationships between the evolution of ERP systems and IS integration or disintegration. In this typology, some examples are provided to illustrate our findings.

Legend: kind of IS evolution – "IS Integration (I)"; – "IS Disintegration (D)".

Combination between research factors in 2014	IS evolution (Examples in relationship with Table 1.2)		
	1998	2014	IS integration or disintegration
E.g. 1.1: ECCO+ & TDEV+ & PMER+& INTE= 0 & ESES– & COER+ & ESEV+ = internal development	ERP 1st G (IS No.2)	ERP 2nd G (IS No. 1)	TIIS to TIIS (I)
E.g. 1.2: ECCO+ & TDEV– & PMER– & INTE– & ESES– & COER– & ESEV – or + = external acquisition	ERP 1st G (IS No. 2)	IS No. 5, 8 or 9	TIIS to HIIS (D)
E.g. 2.1: ECCO+ & TDEV– & PMER+ & INTE+ & ESES– = simple existing & COER+ & ESEV+	IS No. 4 (DIS)	IS No. 7 or 8	DIS to HIIS (I)
E.g. 2.2: ECCO+ & TDEV– & PMER– & INTE– & ESES– = complex existing & COER– & ESEV+	IS No. 4 (HIIS)	IS No. 7 or 8	HIIS to DIS (D)
E.g. 3.1: ECCO+ & TDEV– & PMER+ & INTE+ & ESES– = simple existing & COER+ = simple ERP & ESEV+	IS No. 4 (DIS)	IS No. 9	DIS to HIIS (I)
E.g. 3.2: ECCO+ & TDEV– & PMER– & INTE– & ESES– = complex existing & COER– = complex ERP & ESEV+	IS No. 4 (HIIS)	IS No. 9	HIIS to DIS (D)
E.g. 4: ECCO + & TDEV– & PMER– & INTE+ or – & ESES– = complex existing & COER– & ESEV– = keeping an ERP 1st G without any expansion towards a 2nd G or by going out of business	ERP 1st G (IS No.2)	IS No. 9	TIIS to HIIS or to DIS (D)
E.g. 5: ECCO+ & TDEV+ & PMER+ & ESES– or + & COER+ & ESEV+ = internal development	IS No. 3, 4, 5, 6, 7, 8 or 9	ERP 2nd G (IS No. 1)	DIS or HIIS to TIIS (I)

Table 7.1. *Typology of combination of research factors affecting the relationships between the evolution of ERP systems and IS integration or disintegration*

Example 1: an IS that evolves from ERP 1st to 2nd G and that is sold by the same vendor *(Example 1.1)* is defined by the combination (ECCO+ & TDEV+ & PMER+ & INTE=0 & ESES– & COER+ & ESEV+ = internal development) as values of the research factors promoting IS integration by keeping a kind of TIIS (the IS evolution, to fit with clients' needs, allows maintenance of the same initial integration rate (see Table 1.3). However, an IS evolution that combines an ERP system with third-party software: Best of Breed or other *(Example 1.2)* sets the combination (ECCO+ & TDEV– & PMER– & INTE– & ESES– & COER– & ESEV– or + = external acquisition) as values of the research factors promoting IS disintegration (return from a TIIS to an HIIS). The difference between these two IS evolutions *(Examples 1.1 and 1.2)* can be explained by the changing of the values of the following factors: TDEV, PMER, INTE, COER and ESEV.

Example 2: the nature of the legacy systems (simple or complex) on which urbanization has been conducted can also impact the relationship between the evolution of ERP systems and IS integration or disintegration. The integration from a DIS to an HIIS *(Example 2.1)* could be the result of the following combination in 2014: (ECCO+ & TDEV– & PMER+ & INTE+ & ESES– = simple existing & COER+ & ESEV+); while the disintegration from an HIIS to a DIS *(Example 2.2)* could be the product of the following combination: (ECCO+ & TDEV– & PMER– & INTE– & ESES– = complex existing & COER– & ESEV+). The difference between these two IS evolutions *(Examples 2.1 and 2.2)* can be explained by the changing of the values of the following factors: PMER, INTE, ESES and COER.

Example 3: the ERP system complexity or simplicity can also guide the orientation of IS integration or disintegration. The integration from a DIS to an HIIS *(Example 3.1)* can be the result of the following combination: (ECCO+ & TDEV– & PMER+ & INTE+ & ESES– = simple existing system & COER+ = simple ERP & ESEV+); while the disintegration from an HIIS to a DIS *(Example 3.2)* could be the product of the following combination: (ECCO + & TDEV– & PMER– & INTE– & ESES– = complex existing system & COER- = complex ERP & ESEV+). The difference between these two IS evolutions *(Examples 3.1 and 3.2)* can be explained by the changing of the values of the following factors: PMER, INTE, ESES and COER.

Example 4: a company whose IS was composed of PeopleSoft or J.D. Edwards (which were bought by Oracle) does not desire to evolve its legacy system in cooperation with Oracle. The IS can undergo a disintegration by evolving from a TIIS (IS No. 2) to an HIIS or to DIS (IS No. 9). The disintegration can be the result of the combination of the following factors: (ECCO + & TDEV– & PMER– & INTE + or – & ESES– = complex existing & COER– & ESEV– = keeping an ERP 1st G without any expansion toward a 2nd G or by the vendor going out of business).

Example 5: the integration from a DIS or an HIIS (IS No. 3, 4, 5, 6, 7, 8 or 9) to a TIIS (IS No. 1) could be the result of the following combination: (ECCO+ & TDEV+ & PMER+ & ESES– or + & COER+ & ESEV+ = internal development). Other examples can also be given. We let the readers deduce other possible combinations.

8

Interests and Limitations of the Research

This chapter explains the strength and weakness of this research. It also suggests some search tracks and some refinements for future research which could be interesting in order to complete this work.

The added value of this book is to show how a possible IS disintegration, instead of a desired integration, could happen due to the evolution of enterprise resource planning (ERP) systems. This idea, which, according to our knowledge, has not been studied before, can indicate the direction of new paths of research. As a result, this book could be considered to be a foundation on which to build, in the future, wide-ranging research in the field of the relationships between the evolution of ERP systems and information system (IS) integration or disintegration.

This book could be useful for researchers, teachers and students as part of their analysis and understanding related to the role, contribution and position of the ERP system within the whole IS. In the coming years, our work may also be interesting for the research and development led by vendors to better guide the evolution of their ERP systems. All stakeholders (firms, IS managers, consultants, consulting firms, information technology (IT) companies and project teams, etc.) could also find in this book the type of best practices that can help them in the exercise of their profession.

This study, does, however, have several limitations. First, our choice of research factors affecting the relationships between the evolution of ERP systems and IS integration or disintegration may not be exhaustive. In fact, our choices were focused on the factors that we have considered to be significant in relation to our research question in today's context. Second, there was a paucity of literature to review in the field of the IS disintegration, which did not allow us to have the necessary foundation to write a wide-ranging research book. Third, we did not address a statistical analysis in this research, which was limited to a qualitative research method. Consequently, for all of these reasons, the generalizability of the findings may be limited.

Based on these limitations, we would like to propose refinements for future research. As we were looking in this book to highlight some new tendencies in the progress of evolution, for which a certain amount of observation is necessary, our study needs to be completed. Therefore, other complementary research, especially longitudinal and statistical analysis, will be interesting in the future.

Conclusion

The conclusion covers the main result that might shape the relationships between the evolution of enterprise resource planning (ERP) packages and information systems (ISs). It also provides two tables (Tables C.1 and C.2) of useful best practices in this field:

– Table C.1: the impact of the research factors on the relationships between the evolution of ERP systems and IS integration or disintegration;

– Table C.2: relationships between the combinations of the research factor values and IS integration or disintegration.

From the literature review, we conducted an analysis of the relationship between the evolution of ERP systems and current trends in the field of ISs. Although previous studies have shown the role of ERP systems in IS integration, we proposed a new track of research aimed to prove that in some cases, the evolution of these packages can lead to a kind of IS disintegration instead of the intended integration.

We found that links between ERP systems and ISs are triggered by certain variables or factors: economic crisis and competitiveness, total dependency on the ERP vendors, project management, interoperability and complexity of the ERP systems, evolution strategies of existing systems and of ERP vendors. Three case studies have confirmed the relevance of these variables as well as the validity of the two values (positive and negative) given to each of them.

This book has established cause/effect links between the evolution of ERP systems and IS integration or disintegration, which can be activated by the values taken by the research factors. We have developed a typology (see Table 7.1) that has summarized several scenarios leading the architectures to either integration or to disintegration. This typology has emphasized the importance of these factors that play a pivotal role in determining the impact of the evolution of ERP systems on IS integration or disintegration.

Although the ERP system's implementation is logically a factor aiming to improve the IS integration, the negative values of the research factors could prevent this integration. These negative values, that are related to the ERP system's evolution, could also cause a kind of IS regression from a state of integration toward one of disintegration. The following table summarizes the interactions between the research factors, the evolution of ERP systems and IS integration or disintegration.

Research factors	IS disintegration	IS integration
Economic crisis and competitiveness (ECCO)	The economic crisis and competitiveness are not taken into account by all stakeholders as an important factor within the framework of ERP system evolution. ERP system prices are too expensive for clients. The TCO of an ERP system is very costly in a manner that does not allow firms to be competitive, especially within the context of economic crisis. Consequently, TCO could be an obstacle which prevents a firm from acquiring an ERP system, and thus this obstacle cannot help IS integration. **The value of ECCO is "–"**	The economic crisis and competitiveness are carefully taken into account by all stakeholders as an important factor within the framework of ERP system evolution. ERP vendors, within the context of an economic crisis, democratize the prices. The TCO of ERP systems becomes attractive in a manner that allows firms: (1) to make the decision of "go" (buying an ERP system) instead of "no go"; (2) to be competitive and to win an add-value, due to the ERP package, especially within the context of economic crisis. **The value of ECCO is "+"**
Total Dependency on the ERP Vendors (TDEV)	The evolution of ERP systems takes into account this factor in a manner that allows the client to decide whether to be independent or dependent on an ERP vendor. Consequently, the client could be independent of an ERP vendor. **The value of TDEV is "–"**	The evolution of ERP systems takes into account this factor in a manner that does not allow the client to decide whether to be independent or dependent on an ERP vendor. Consequently, the client is completely dependent on the ERP vendor. **The value of TDEV is "+"**

Project Management ERP (PMER)	The evolution of ERP systems does not take into account this factor in a manner which allows improvement or optimization of ERP system project management. A methodology for ERP system implementation, based on best practices, is not taken into account by all stakeholders as an important factor within the framework of ERP system evolution. **The value of PMER is "–"**	The evolution of ERP systems takes into account this factor in a manner that allows improvement or optimization of ERP system project management. A methodology for ERP system implementation, based on best practices, is taken into account by all stakeholders as an important factor within the framework of ERP system evolution. **The value of PMER is "+"**
Interoperability of the ERP (INTE)	The evolution of ERP systems does not take into account this factor in a manner that allows improvement of the ERP system interoperability. Consequently, clients are not able to integrate the different subsystems of their IS. **The value of INTE is "–"**	The evolution of ERP systems takes into account this factor in a manner that allows improvement of the ERP system interoperability. Consequently, clients are able to integrate easily the different subsystems of their IS. **The value of INTE is "+"**
Evolution Strategy of Existing Systems (ESES)	The evolution of ERP systems does not take into account this factor in a manner that allows the firm to drive the best evolution strategy depending on its existing system (urbanization or total overhaul). For example: a desired urbanization that aims to implement an ERP system within the framework of a complex existing system, could be difficult to achieve if the ERP system is complex and its interoperability is unreliable (a total overhaul will be indispensable to avoid IS disintegration). **The value of ESES is "– = complex existing system".**	The evolution of ERP systems takes into account this factor in a manner that allows the firm to drive the best evolution strategy depending on its existing system (urbanization or total overhaul). For example: (1) total overhaul could be performed especially when the existing system is extremely complex; (2) urbanization could be preferred when the existing system is simple or could be avoided when the existing system is complex. **The value of ESES is "+" or "– = simple existing system".**
COER (COmplexity of ERP)	The evolution of ERP systems does not take into account this factor in a manner that allows simplification of the ERP system's complexity. **The value of COER is "–"**	The evolution of ERP systems takes into account this factor in a manner that allows simplification of the ERP system's complexity. **The value of COER is "+"**

Evolution Strategy of ERP Vendors (ESEV)	The evolution of ERP systems does not take into account this factor in a manner that allows the vendors to achieve a relevant evolution from an ERP 1st G to an ERP 2nd G that can fit the users' needs. The ERP 1st G is kept without any expansion toward a 2nd G or by the vendor going out of business. Clients could have a lot of difficulties if they decide to maintain this ERP 1st G within the framework of their IS. **The value of ESEV is "–"**	The evolution of ERP systems takes into account this factor in a manner that allows the vendors to achieve a relevant evolution from an ERP 1st G to an ERP 2nd G that can fit the users' needs. Clients could be more or less interested in an ERP 2nd G according to a given evolution strategy (internal development or external acquisition). For example: (1) the upgrading process does not dissuade the client to buy an ERP system because of its future upgrading's significant costs; (2) simplification of the upgrading process from 1st to 2nd G which could lead, if it is possible, to an ERP 2nd G whose future upgrading will not be complex. **The value of ESEV is "+"**

Table C.1. *The impact of the research factors on the relationships between the evolution of ERP systems and IS integration or disintegration*

Just as the value (positive or negative) taken by each factor can impact the ERP system's evolution on the IS (toward integration or disintegration), the combination of this same value with the values of other factors could also modify these outcomes. Generally, we found that it is not clear enough or reliable enough to consider a single factor alone. To have a reliable and complete perspective, it is better to take each factor in combination with other factors. The following table illustrates the contribution of the combinations of the research factors values in determining of the relationships between ERP systems' evolution and IS integration or disintegration.

In the future, we think that ERP system evolution will not be a matter for vendors only. All stakeholders (firms, vendors, consultants, consultancy firms, etc.) should participate in and contribute to this evolution. A solution that takes into account all of the stakeholders' points of view could better improve IS integration. Without this coordination, a kind of IS disintegration, triggered by the ERP system's evolution, could occur.

Research factors	Values		
ECCO	–	Between – and +	+
TDEV	–	Between – and +	+
PMER	–	Between – and +	+
INTE	–	Between – and +	+
ESES	– = complex existing.	Between – and +	+
COER	–	Between – and +	+
ESEV	–	Between – and +	+
Integration rate of IS	DIIS	HIIS	TIIS

Table C.2. *Relationships between the combinations of the research factor values and IS integration or disintegration*

IS integration could be improved by ERP systems if their evolution is driven in a manner that promotes the rational selection of a package and their purchase by clients, which then also guarantees the success of their implementation. IS disintegration, however, could be provoked due to ERP systems if their evolution is driven in a manner that does not encourage clients to select packages rationally or to purchase them, which works against the success of their implementation.

Finally, an ERP implementation does not automatically mean the improvement of the integration of information systems. In certain cases and under some conditions this implementation could instead provoke a kind of disintegration. All stakeholders should be careful to avoid this undesired scenario which can lead to the disintegration of the information system instead of its integration.

Bibliography

[ABE 06] ABERDEEN GROUP, Best practices in extending ERP, Research brief, November, 2006.

[ABE 07] ABERDEEN GROUP, The total cost of ERP ownership, Research brief, July 2007.

[ABE 08] ABERDEEN GROUP, The ERP in manufacturing benchmark report, June 2008.

[ABE 09] ABERDEEN GROUP, The ERP in action: Epicor, June 2009.

[AKK 02] AKKERMANS H.A., HELDEN K.V., "Vicious and virtuous cycles in ERP implementation: a case study of interrelations between critical success factors", *European Journal of Information Systems*, vol. 11, pp. 35–46, 2002.

[AKK 03] AKKERMANS H.A., BOGERD P., YÜCESAN E. *et al.*, "The impact of ERP on supply chain management: exploratory findings from a European Delphi study", *European Journal of Operational Research*, vol. 146, pp. 284–301, 2003.

[ALA 01] ALADWANI A.M., "Change management strategies for successful ERP implementation", *Business Process Management Journal*, vol. 7, no. 3, pp. 266–275, 2001.

[ALM 00a] AL-MASHARI M., ZAIRI M., "Revisiting BPR: a holistic review of practice and development", *Business Process Management Journal*, vol. 6, no. 1, pp. 10–42, 2000.

[ALM 00b] AL-MASHARI M., "Enterprise-wide information systems: the case of SAP R/3 application", in *Proceedings of the 2nd International Conference on Enterprise Information Systems*, pp. 3–8, 2000.

[ALM 01] AL-MUDIMIGH A., ZAIRI M., AL-MASHARI M., "ERP software implementation: an integrative framework", *European Journal of Information Systems*, vol. 10, no. 4, pp. 216–226, 2001.

[ALM 03] AL-MASHARI M., AL-MUDIMIGH A., ZAIRI M., "Enterprise resource planning: a taxonomy of critical factors", *European Journal of Operational Research*, vol. 146, no. 2, pp. 352–364, 2003.

[ALM 06] AL-MASHARI M., GHANI S.K., AL-RASHID W., "A study of the critical success factors of ERP implementation in developing countries", *International Journal of Internet and Enterprise Management*, vol. 4, no. 1, pp. 68–95, 2006.

[ALO 07] ALOINI D., DULMIN R., MININNO V., "Risk management in ERP project introduction: review of the literature", *Information & Management*, vol. 44, no. 6, pp. 547–567, available at http://dx.doi.org/10.1016/j.im.2007.05.004, 2007.

[ALV 00] ALVAREZ R., "Examining an ERP implementation through myths: a case study of a large public organization", *Proceedings of the Americas Conference of Information Systems*, Long Beach, California, pp. 1655–1661, 2000.

[AMR 97] AMR RESEARCH, Enterprise resource planning software report, 1997–2002, Boston, Massachusetts, 1997.

[AND 79] ANDERSON J., NARASIMHAN R., "Assessing implementation risk: a technological approach", *Management Science*, vol. 25, pp. 512–521, 1979.

[AND 97] ANDERSON E.E., CHEN Y.-M., "Microcomputer software evaluation: an econometric model", *Decision Support Systems*, vol. 19, no. 2, pp. 75–92, 1997.

[ANE 06] ANEXINET R.B., Top 10 ERP implementation pitfalls, retrieved 11th February 2010, available at http://www.anexinet.com/pdfs/ERP_top10pitfalls3-2006.pdf, 2006.

[ANI 01] ANIDJAR J., "Nous nous intéressons aux standards quand ils deviennent des réalités opérationnelles", *JDNet*, 9 May 2001.

[AYA 07] AYAĞ Z., OZDEMIR R.G., "An intelligent approach to ERP software selection through fuzzy ANP", *International Journal of Production Research*, vol. 45, no. 10, pp. 2169–2194, 2007.

[BAC 96] BACHARACH S.B., BAMBERGER P., SONNENSTUHL W.J., "The organizational transformation process: the micro politics of dissonance reduction and the alignment of logics of action", *Administrative Science Quarterly*, vol. 41, pp. 477–506, 1996.

[BAR 93] BARKI H., RIVERD S., TALBOT J., "Toward an assessment of software development risk", *Journal of Management Information Systems*, vol. 10, no. 2, pp. 203–225, 1993.

[BAR 02] BARKI H., PINSONNEAULT A., "Explaining ERP implementation effort and benefits with organizational integration", *Cahier du Gresi*, vol. 20, no. 1, p. 54, 2002.

[BAR 05] BARKI H., PINSONNEAULT A., "A model of organizational integration, implementation effort, and performance", *Organization Science*, vol. 16 no. 2, pp. 165–179, 2005.

[BAX 08] BAXTER P., JACK S., "Qualitative case study methodology: study design and implementation for novice researchers", *The Qualitative Report*, vol. 13, no. 4, pp. 544–559, available at https://www.nova.edu/ssss/QR/QR13-4/baxter.pdf, 2008.

[BER 01] BERNROIDER E., KOCH S., "ERP selection process in midsize and large organizations", *Business Process Management Journal*, vol. 7, no. 3, pp. 251–257, 2001.

[BER 02] BERETT S., "Unleashing the integration potential of ERP systems: the role of process-based performance measurement systems", *Business Process Management Journal*, vol. 8, no. 3, pp. 254–277, 2002.

[BER 05] BERCHET C., HABCHI G., "The implementation and deployment of an ERP system: an industrial case study", *Computers in Industry*, vol. 56, no. 6, pp. 588–605, 2005.

[BID 04a] BIDAN M., ROWE F., "Urbanization practices and strategic behavior: openness of architecture and enactment in two medium sized companies", *IXème Colloque AIM*, INT Evry, 2004.

[BID 04b] BIDAN M., "Fédération et intégration des applications du système d'information de gestion", *Système d'Information et Management*, vol. 9, no. 2, pp. 5–14, 2004.

[BID 12] BIDAN M., ROWE F., TRUEX D., "An empirical study of IS architectures in French SMEs: integration approaches", *European Journal of Information Systems*, vol. 21, no. 3, pp. 287–302, 2012.

[BIN 99] BINGI P., SHARMA M.K., GODLA J.K., "Critical issues affecting an ERP implementation", *Information Systems Management*, vol. 16, no. 3, pp. 7–14, 1999.

[BIS 09] BISCOTTI F., Report highlight for market trends: enterprise software, EMEA, 2008-2013, available at http://www.gartner.com/DisplayDocument?ref=g_search&id=938713&subref=browse, 28 May 2009.

[BOU 03] BOURDEAU S., RIVARD S., BARKI H., "Évaluation du risque en gestion de projets", *Série scientifique*, vol. 47, p. 54, CIRANO, Montreal, available at http://www.cirano.qc.ca/pdf/publication/2003s-47.pdf, 2003.

[BOW 98] BOWERSOX D.J., CLOSS D.J., HALL C.T., "Beyond ERP – the storm before the calm", *Supply Chain Management Review*, vol. 1, no. 4, pp. 28–37, 1998.

[BRA 03] BRADFORD M., FLORIN J., "Examining the role of innovation diffusion factors on the implementation success of enterprise resource planning systems", *International Journal of Accounting Information Systems*, vol. 4, pp. 205–225, 2003.

[BRA 08] BRADLEY J., "Management based critical success factors in the implementation of enterprise resource planning systems", *International Journal of Accounting Information Systems*, vol. 9, no. 3, pp. 175–200, 2008.

[BRO 81] BROWN R.M., STEPHENSON K., "The evaluation of purchased computer software", *Mid-South Business Journal*, vol. 7, pp. 8–11, 1981.

[BRO 95] BRODIE M., STONEBRAKER M., *Migrating Legacy Systems Gateways, Interfaces and the Incremental Approach*, Morgan Kaufmann Publishers, Inc., 1995.

[BRO 99] BROWN C., VESSEY I., "ERP Implementation Approaches: Toward a Contingency Framework", *Proceedings of the* 20th *International Conference on Information Systems,* pp. 411–416, December 1999.

[BUE 08] BUENO S., SALMERON J.L., "Fuzzy modeling enterprise resource planning tool selection", *Computer Standards and Interfaces*, vol. 30, no. 3, pp. 137–147, 2008.

[BUL 96] BULKELEY W.M., "A cautionary network tale: Fox-Meyer's high-tech gamble", *Wall Street Journal Interactive Edition*, 18 November 1996.

[CAL 98] CALDWELL B., STEIN T., "Beyond ERP – new IT agenda – a second wave of ERP activity promises to increase efficiency and transform ways of doing business", *Information Week*, vol. 711, pp. 34–35, 30 November 1998.

[CAM 06] CAMPBELL I., "SAP at the centre of internet maelstrom over Ad campaign", *FSN Business Systems News & Analysis for Finance and IT Professionals*, available at http://www.fsn.co.uk/channel_enterprise_financials/ sap_at_the_centre_of_internet_maelstrom_over_ad_campaign, 2006.

[CAN 99] CANTU R., A framework for implementing enterprise resource planning systems in small manufacturing companies, Master's thesis, St. Mary's University, San Antonio, Texas, 1999.

[CAR 00] CARLINO J., NELSON S., SMITH N., AMR research study reveals SAP R/3 upgrade cost users 25 to 33 percent of initial investment, available at: http://www.amrresearch.com/pressroom/files/00426.asp, 2000.

[CAR 04] CARR N., *Does it Matter? Information Technology and the Corrosion of Competitive Advantage*, Harvard Business School Press, Boston, 2004.

[CHA 95] CHAU P.Y.K., "Factors used in the selection of packaged software in small businesses: views of owners and managers", *Information and Management*, vol. 29, no. 2, pp. 71–78, 1995.

[CHE 01] CHEN I.J., "Planning for ERP systems: analysis and future trend", *Business Process Management Journal*, vol. 7, no. 5, pp. 374–386, 2001.

[CHE 08a] CHEN D., DOUMEINGTS G., VERNADAT F., "Architectures for enterprise integration and interoperability: past, present and future", *Computers in Industry*, vol. 59, pp. 647–659, 2008.

[CHE 08b] CHEN R., SUN C., HELMS M.M. *et al.*, "Role negotiation and interaction: an exploratory case study of the impact of management consultants on ERP system implementation in SMEs in Taiwan", *Information Systems Management*, vol. 25, no. 2, pp. 159–73, 2008.

[CHE 09] CHEN H.-H., CHEN C.-S., TSAI L.H., "A study of successful ERP – from the organization fit perspective", *Journal of Systemics, Cybernetics and Informatics*, vol. 7, no. 4, pp. 8–16, 2009.

[CHU 11] CHUNG S.H., TANG H.-L., AHMAD I., "Modularity, integration and IT personnel skills factors in linking ERP to SCM systems", *Journal of Technology Management & Innovation*, vol. 6, pp. 1–3, 2011.

[CIB 00] CIBORRA C., BRAA K., CORDELLA A. *et al.*, *From Control to Drift – the Dynamics of Corporate Information Infrastructures*, Oxford University Press, Oxford, 2000.

[CIG 03] CIGREF., La Gouvernance du sytème d'information, Internal report CIGREF, available at http:// www.cigref.fr, 2003.

[COL 04] COLMENARES L.E., "Critical success factors of enterprise resource planning systems implementation in Venezuela", *Americas Conference on Information Systems (AMCIS) Proceedings paper 21*, pp. 134–139, 2004.

[COM 98] COMPUTERGRAM INTERNATIONAL, Fox Meyer plus two sue Andersen for SAP Snafus, available at http://www.bnetaustralia.com.au, 20 July 1998.

[CUR 98] CURRAN T., KELLER G., *SAP R/3 Business Blueprint: Understanding the Business Process Reference Model*, Prentice Hall, 1998.

[DAV 98] DAVENPORT T.H., "Putting the enterprise into the enterprise system", *Harvard Business Review*, vol. 76, no. 4, pp. 121–131, 1998.

[DAV 00] DAVENPORT T.H., *Mission Critical: Realizing the Promise of Enterprise Systems*, Harvard Business School Press, Boston, MA, 2000.

[DAV 01] DAVENPORT T.H., HARRIS J.G., DELONG D.W. *et al.*, "Data to knowledge to results: building an analytical capability", *California Management Review*, vol. 43, no. 2, pp. 117–138, 2001.

[DAV 04] DAVENPORT T.H., HARRIS J.G., CANTRELL S., "Enterprise systems and ongoing process change", *Business Process Management Journal*, vol. 10, no. 1, pp. 16–26, 2004.

[DAV 05] DAVENPORT T.H., *Thinking For a Living: How to Get Better Performances and Results from Knowledge Workers Hardcover*, Harvard Business Review Press, 13 September 2005.

[DES 04] DESHAYES C., "Progiciels de gestion intégrés, le temps du bilan?", *JDNet*, March 2004.

[DEU 98] DEUTSCH C., "Software that can make a grown company cry", *The New York Times*, vol. 148, no. 51, pp. 1–13, 1998.

[DIE 98] DIEDERICH T., *Bankrupt Firm Blames SAP for Failure*, Computer World, 28 August 1998.

[DIX 11] DIXIT, ASHISH K., PRAKASH O., "Study of issues affecting ERP implementation in SMEs", *International Refereed Research Journal*, vol. 2, no. 2, available at: www.researchersworlld.com, pp. 77–85, April 2011.

[EIS 89] EISENHARDT K.M., "Making fast strategic decisions in high-velocity environments", *Academy of Management Journal*, vol. 32, pp. 543–576, 1989.

[EIS 07] EISENHARDT K.M., "Theory building from cases: opportunities and challenges", *Academy of Management Journal*, vol. 50, no. 1, pp. 25–32, 2007.

[ELA 03] EL AMRANI R., "Vision organisationnelle cible comme facteur de réussite d'un projet ERP: le cas SAP chez l'entreprise Consto", *8ème colloque de l'AIM*, Grenoble, 2003.

[ELA 07] EL AMRANI R., "Le rôle de la conduite du changement dans le succès d'un ERP à Air France," *Gérer et comprendre*, no. 90, pp. 67–81, 2007.

[ELL 10] ELLISON L., Co-founder of Oracle Corporation, 2010.

[ELS 08] EL SAWAH S., EL FATTAH A.A., THARWAT A. *et al.*, "A quantitative model to predict the Egyptian ERP implementation success index", *Business Process Management Journal*, vol. 14, no. 3, pp. 288–306, 2008.

[ESC 99] ESCALLE C.X., COTTELEER M.J., AUSTIN R.D., *Enterprise Resource Planning (ERP): Technology Note*, Harvard Business School Publishing, Boston, MA, 1999.

[EST 01] ESTEVES J., PASTOR J.A., "Analysis of Critical Success Factors Relevance Along SAP Implementation Phases", *Seventh Americas Conference on Information Systems*, pp. 1019–1025, 2001.

[EVE 00] EVERDINGEN Y., HILLERGERSBERG J., WAARTS E., "ERP adoption by European midsize companies", *Communications of the ACM*, vol. 43, no. 4, pp. 27–31, 2000.

[EWU 97] EWUSI-MENSAH K., "Critical issues in abandond information systems development projects". *Communications of the Association for Computing Machinery (ACM)*, vol. 40, no. 9, pp. 74–80, 1997.

[FED 09] FEDERICI T., "Factors influencing ERP outcomes in SMEs: a post-introduction assessment", *Journal of Enterprise Information Management*, Google Scholar, vol. 22, nos. 1–2, pp. 81–98, 2009.

[FIN 07] FINNEY S., CORBETT M., "ERP implementation: a compilation and analysis of critical success factors", *Business Process Management Journal*, vol. 13, no. 3, pp. 329–347, 2007.

[FIS 04] FISHER D.M., FISHER S.A., KIANG M.Y. *et al.*, "Evaluating mid-level ERP software", *Journal of Computer Information Systems*, vol. 45, no. 1, pp. 38–46, 2004.

[FIS 11] FISTER GALE S., "Failure rates finally drop", *PM Network*, pp. 10–11, available at http://www.sbsgroup.usa.com, August 2011.

[FLE 08] FLECHAUX R., "Hausse des coûts de maintenance : SAP sonne la retraite", *LeMagIT: l'informatique pour et par les pros*, available on http://www.lemagit.fr/actualites/2240197428/Hausse-des-couts-de-maintenance-SAP-sonne-la-retraite, 2008.

[FRE 04] FREEMAN, R. E., WICKS, A. C., PARMAR, B., "Stakeholder theory and the Corporate Objective Revisited", *Organization Science*, vol. 15, no. 3, pp. 364–369, http://dx.doi.org/10.1287/orsc.1040.0066, 2004.

[GAB 03] GABLE G., "Consultants and knowledge management", *Journal of Global Information Management*, vol. 11, no. 3, pp. 1–4, 2003.

[GAR 05] GARGEYA V.B., BRADY C., "Success and failure factor of adopting SAP in ERP system implementation", *Business Process Management Journal*, vol. 11, no. 5, pp. 501–516, 2005.

[GAU 07] GAURON M.T., ERP: entre standard et spécifique, un équilibre délicat, Interview, JDNet Solutions, available at http://www.journaldunet.com/solutions/0701/070108-erp-standard-specifique.shtml, May 2007.

[GIB 99] GIBSON N., HOLLAND C., LIGHT B., "A case study of a fast track SAP R/3 implementation at Guilbert", *Electronic Markets*, vol. 9, no. 3, pp. 190–193, June 1999.

[GLA 98] GLASS R.L., "Enterprise resource planning: breakthrough and/or term problem?", *Data Base*, vol. 29, no. 2, pp. 14–15, 1998.

[GOL 91] GOLDENBERG B., "Analyze key factors when choosing software", *Marketing News*, vol. 25, p. 23, 1991.

[GRA 03] GRABSKI S.V., LEECH S.A., LU B., "Enterprise systems implementation risks and controls," in SHANKS G., SEDDON P.B., WILLCOCKS L.P. (eds), *Second-Wave Enterprise Resource Planning Systems: Implementing for Effectiveness*, Cambridge University Press, 2003.

[GRI 98] GRIFFITHS T.D., BÜCHEL C., FRACKOWIAK R.S.J. *et al.*, "Analysis of temporal structure in sound by the human brain", *Nature Neuroscience*, vol. 1, no. 5, pp. 422–427, 1998.

[GRI 99] GRIFFITH T.L., ZAMMUTO R.F., AIMAN-SMITH L., "Why new technologies fail?", *Industrial Management*, vol. 41, no. 3, 1999.

[HAM 99] HAMMER M., STANTON S., "How process enterprises really work", *Harvard Business Review*, vol. 77, no. 6, pp. 108–118, November–December 1999.

[HAN 01] HANSETH O., CIBORRA C.U., BRAA K., "The control devolution. ERP and the side effects of globalization", *The data base for advances in information systems*, vol. 32, no. 4, pp. 34–46, 2001.

[HAN 04] HAN S.W., "ERP-enterprise resource planning: a cost-based business case and implementation assessment", *Human Factors and Ergonomics in Manufacturing*, vol. 14, no. 3, pp. 239–256, 2004.

[HAN 06] HANSETH O., JACUCCI E., GRISOT M. *et al.*, "Reflexive standardization: side effects and complexity in standard making", *MIS Quarterly*, Special issue August–Supplement, vol. 30, pp. 563–581, 2006.

[HEC 97] HECHT B., "Choose the right ERP software", *Datamation*, vol. 43, no. 3, pp. 56–58, 1997.

[HIC 10] HICKEY K., California county dumps SAP, available at http://washingtontechnology.com/articles/2010/08/25/california-county-dumps-sap.aspx, 20 October 2010.

[HIL 05] HILLESTAD R., BIGELOW J., BOWER A. *et al.*, "Can electronic medical record systems transform health care? Potential health benefits, savings, and costs", *Health Affairs*, vol. 24, no. 5, pp. 1103–1117, 2005.

[HIT 02] HITT L.M., WU D.J., ZHOU X., "Investment in enterprise resource planning: business impact and productivity measures", *Journal of Management Information Systems*, vol. 19, no. 1, pp. 71–98, 2002.

[HOL 99] HOLLAND C., LIGHT B., "A critical success factors model for ERP implementation", *IEEE Software*, vol. 16, no. 3, pp. 30–36, May–June 1999.

[HON 02] HONGK K., KIM Y.-G., "The critical success factors for ERP implementation: an organizational fit perspective", *Information and Management*, vol. 40, no. 1, pp. 25–40, 2002.

[HOP 08] HOPKINS R., JENKINS K., *Eating the IT Elephant: Moving from Greenfield Development to Brownfield*, IBM Press, Upper Saddle River, NJ, 2008.

[HSI 04] HSIUJU R.Y., CHWEN S., "Aligning ERP implementation with competitive priorities of manufacturing firms: an exploratory study", *International Journal of Production Economics*, vol. 92, pp. 207–220, 2008.

[HYV 03] HYVONEN T., "Management accounting and information systems – ERP vs BoB", *European Accounting Review*, vol. 12, no. 1, pp. 155–173, available at http://ssrn.com/abstract=369323, 2003.

[IBR 08] IBRAHIM A.M.S., SHARP J.M., SYNTETOS A.A., "A framework for the implementation of ERP to improve business performance: a case study", in IRANI Z., SAHRAOUI S., GHONEIM A. *et al.* (eds), *Proceedings of the European and Mediterranean Conference on Information Systems (EMCIS)*, 2008.

[IRA 03] IRANI Z., THEMISTOCLEOUS M., LOVE P.E.D., "The impact of enterprise application integration on information system lifecycles", *Information and Management*, vol. 41, no. 2, pp. 177–188, 2003.

[JAM 05] JAMISON T.A., LAYMAN P.A., NISKA B.T. *et al.*, *Evaluation of Enterprise Architecture Interoperability*, Air Force Institute of Technology, Ohio, 2005.

[JAR 00] JARRAR Y.F., AL-MUDIMIGH A., ZAIRI M., "ERP implementation critical success factors-the role and impact of business process management", *International Conference on Management of Innovation and Technology*, vol. 1, pp. 122–127, 2000.

[JES 97] JESITUS J., "Broken promises?; FoxMeyer's project was a disaster. Was the company too aggressive or was it misled?", *Industry Week*, pp. 31–37, 3 November 1997.

[JIA 99] JIANG J.J., KLEIN G., "Risks to different aspects of system success", *Information and Management*, vol. 36, pp. 263–272, 1999.

[JOH 07] JOHANSSON B., Why focus on roles when developing future ERP systems, available at: www.3gerp.org, 2007.

[KAL 03] KALLING T., "ERP systems and the strategic management processes that lead to competitive advantage", *Information Resources Management Journal*, vol. 16, no. 4, pp. 46–67, 2003.

[KAM 08] KAMHAWI E.M., "Enterprise resource-planning systems adoption in Bahrain: motives, benefits, and barriers", *Journal of Enterprise Information Management*, vol. 21, no. 3, pp. 310–334, 2008.

[KAN 11] KANARACUS C., Epicor sued over alleged ERP project failure, Computer world, available at http://www.computerworld.com, 11 August 2011.

[KEI 06] KEIL M., TIWANA A., "Relative importance of evaluation criteria for enterprise systems: a conjoint study", *Information Systems Journal*, vol. 16, no. 3, pp. 237–262, 2006.

[KEI 95] KEIL M., "Pulling the plug: software project management and the problem of project escalation", *Management Information Systems Quarterly*, vol. 19, no. 4, pp. 421–447, December 1995.

[KHO 06] KHOUMBATI K., THEMISTOCLEOUS M., IRANI Z., "Evaluating the adoption of enterprise application integration in healthcare organizations", *Journal Management Information System*, vol. 22, no. 4, pp. 69–108, 2006.

[KHO 07] KHOLEIF A.O., ABDEL-KADER M., SHERER M., "ERP customization failure: Institutionalized accounting practices, power relations and market forces", *Journal of Accounting and Organizational Change*, vol. 3, pp. 250–269, 2007.

[KIM 06] KIMBERLING E., 7 critical success factors to make your ERP or IT project successful, available at http://it.toolbox.com/blogs/erp-roi/7-criticalsuccess-factors-to-make-your-erp-or-it-project-successful-12058, 2006.

[KIM 11] KIMBERLING E., Back to school: when will ERP software customers learn to avoid failure?, available at http://panorama-consulting.com/back-to-school-when-will-erp-software-customers-learn-to-avoid-failure/, 2011.

[KIN 06] KING S.F., BURGESS T.F., "Beyond critical success factors: A dynamic model of enterprise system innovation", *International Journal of Information Management,* vol. 26, no. 1, pp. 59–69, 2006.

[KON 05] KONSTANTAS D., BOURRIÈRES J.P., LÉONARD M. *et al.*, "Interoperability of enterprise software and applications", *Proceedings of the First Conference on Interoperability of Enterprise Software and Applications, INTEROP-ESA'05*, Springer-Verlag, Geneva, Switzerland, pp. 409–420, 2005.

[KUM 00] KUMAR K., HILLEGERSBERG J.V., "ERP experiences and evolution", *Communications of the ACM*, vol. 43, no. 4, pp. 22–26, 2000.

[KUM 02] KUMAR V., MAHESHWARI B., KUMAR U., "Enterprise resource planning systems adoption process: a survey of Canadian organizations", *International Journal of Production Research*, vol. 40, no. 3, pp. 509–523, 2002.

[KUM 03] KUMAR V., MAHESHWARI B., KUMAR U., "An investigation of critical management issues in ERP implementation: empirical evidence from Canadian organizations", *Technovation*, vol. 23, no. 10, pp. 793–807, 2003.

[KUM 10] KUMAR V., "Application of analytical hierarchy process to prioritize the factors affecting ERP implementation", *International Journal of Computer Applications*, vol. 2, no. 2, pp. 0975–8887, 2010.

[KYU 02] KYUNG-KWON H., YOUNG-GUL K., "The critical success factors for ERP implementation: an organizational fit perspective", *Information & Management*, vol. 40, pp. 25–40, 2002.

[LAL 06] LALL V., TEYARACHAKUL S., "Enterprise resource planning (ERP) system selection: a data envelopment analysis (DEA) approach", *Journal of Computer Information Systems*, vol. 47, no. 1, pp. 123–127, 2006.

[LAM 01] LAMBERT D., "Peu d'entreprises sont prêtes à se lancer dans des chantiers d'urbanisation", *JDNet*, available at http://www.journaldunet.com/solutions/itws/010709_it_lambert.shtml, July, 2001.

[LAN 00] LANGENWALTER G., *Enterprise Resources Planning and Beyond: Integrating Your Entire Organization*, St. Lucie Press, Boca Raton, FL, 2000.

[LAU 99] LAUGHLIN S., "An ERP game plan", *Journal of Business Strategy*, vol. 20, no. 1, pp. 32–37, January–February, 1999.

[LEE 04] LEE C.J., MYERS M.D., "The challenges of enterprise integration: cycles of integration and disintegration over time", *Proceedings of the 25th International Conference on Information Systems*, Washington, D.C., Association for Information Systems, pp. 927–937, 12–15 December 2004.

[LEO 07] LEON A., *ERP Demystified*, McGraw-Hill Education (India) Ltd., 2007.

[LIA 07] LIAO X.W., LI Y., LU B., "A model for selecting an ERP system based on linguistic information processing", *Information Systems*, vol. 32, no. 7, pp. 1005–1017, 2007.

[LIG 01] LIGHT B., HOLLAND C.P., WILLS K., "ERP and best of breed: a comparative analysis", *Business Process Management Journal*, vol. 7, no. 3, pp. 216–224, 2001.

[LIL 04] LI-LING H., MINDER C., "Impacts of ERP systems on the integrated-interaction performance of manufacturing and marketing", *Industrial Management & Data Systems*, vol. 104, no. 1, pp. 42–55, 2004.

[LIN 08] LINDLEY J. T., TOPPING S., LINDLEY L., "The hidden financial costs of ERP Software", *Managerial Finance*, vol. 34, no. 2, pp. 78–90, 2008.

[LON 01] LONGÉPÉ C., *Le Projet d'Urbanisation du Système d'Information – Démarche Pratique avec Cas Concret*, Dunod, 2001.

[LON 09] LONGÉPÉ C., *Le Projet d'Urbanisation du SI: Cas Concret d'Architecture d'Entreprise*, Dunod, Paris, p. 284, 2009.

[MAB 00] MABERT V.A., SONI A., VENKATARAMANAN M.A., "Enterprise resource planning survey of us manufacturing firms", *Production and Inventory Management Journal*, vol. 41, pp. 52–58, 2000.

[MAB 03] MABERT V.A., SONI A., VENKATARAMANAN M.A., "Enterprise resource planning: Managing the implementation process", *European Journal of Operational Research*, vol. 146, no. 2, pp. 302–314, 2003.

[MAC 08] MACKINNON W., GRANT G., CRAY D., "Enterprise information systems and strategic flexibility", *Proceedings of the 41st Hawaii International Conference on System Sciences*, p. 402, 2008.

[MAR 00a] MARKUS M.L., AXLINE S., PETRIE D. *et al.*, "Learning from adopters' experiences with ERP: problems encountered and success achieved", *Journal of Information Technology*, vol. 15, no. 4, pp. 245–265, 2000.

[MAR 00b] MARKUS M.L., PETRIE D., AXLINE S., "Bucking the trends: what the future may hold for ERP packages", *Information Systems Frontiers*, vol. 2, no. 2, pp. 181–193, 2000.

[MAR 00c] MARKUS M.L., TANIS C., FENEMA C., "Multisite ERP implementations", *Communications of the ACM*, vol. 43, no. 4, pp. 42–46, 2000.

[MAR 01] MARKUS M.L., "Reflections on the system integration enterprise", *Business Process Management Journal*, vol. 7, no. 3, pp. 1–9, 2001.

[MCG 09] MCGRAW HILL CONSTRUCTION, SmartMarket Report: The Business Value of BIM -Getting Building Information Modeling to the Bottom Line, New York, available at http://www.ukessays.com/dissertation/examples/construction/building-information-modelling.php, 2007.

[MCK 98] MCKIE S., "Packaged solution or pandora's box?", *Intelligent Enterprise*, pp. 39–43, November 1998.

[MOM 10] MOMOH A., ROY R., SHEHAB E., "Challenges in enterprise resource planning implementation: state-of-the-art", *Business Process Management Journal*, vol. 16, no. 4, pp. 537–564, 2010.

[MON 04] MONTGOMERY N., "Build your business case for upgrades by adding functionality", *Computer Weekly*, p. 16, 2 October 2004.

[MON 96] MONTAZEMI A.R., CAMERON D.A., GUPTA K.M., "An empirical study of factors affecting software package selection", *Journal of Management Information Systems*, vol. 13, no. 1, pp. 89–105, Summer 1996.

[MOO 05] MOON Y.B., PHATAK D., "Enhancing ERP system's functionality with discrete event simulation", *Industrial Management & Data Systems*, vol. 105, no. 9, pp. 1206–1224, 2005.

[MOO 07] MOON Y.B., YOUNG B., "Enterprise resource planning (ERP): a review of the literature", *International Journal of Management and Enterprise Development*, vol. 4, no. 3, pp. 235–264, 2007.

[MOT 02] MOTWANI J., MIRCHANDANI D., MADAN M. *et al.*, "Successful implementation of ERP projects: evidence from two case studies", *International Journal of Production Economics*, vol. 75, no. 1, pp. 83–96, 2002.

[MOT 05] MOTWANI J., SUBRAMANIAN R., GOPALAKRISHNA P., "Critical factors for successful ERP implementation: exploratory findings from four case studies", *Computers in Industry*, vol. 56, no. 6, pp. 529–544, 2005.

[MUS 02] MUSCATELLO J., An exploratory study of the implementation of enterprise resource planning (ERP), Doctoral thesis, Cleveland State University, 2002.

[MUS 06] MUSCATELLO J.R., PARENTE D.H., "Enterprise resource planning (ERP): a post implementation cross-cross analysis", *Information Resource Management Journal*, vol. 3, pp. 61–81, 2006.

[NAH 01] NAH F., FAJA S., CATA T., "Characteristics of ERP software maintenance: a multiple case study", *Journal of Software Maintenance*, vol. 13, no. 6, pp. 1–16, 2001.

[NAH 03] NAH F.F.-H., ZUCKWEILER K.M., LAU J.L.-S., "ERP implementation: chief information officers' perceptions of critical success factors", *International Journal of Human-Computer Interaction*, vol. 16, no. 1, pp. 5–22, 2003.

[NAU 07] NAUGÈS L., Le mot le plus dangereux de la langue informatique?, available at http://nauges.typepad.com/my_weblog/2007/01/index.html, 2007.

[NAU 08] NAUGÈS L., De quoi vous SAPper le moral!, available at http://nauges.typepad.com/my_weblog/2008/07/de-quoi-vous-sapper-le-moral.html, 2008.

[NEL 99] NELSON E., RAMSTAD E., "Hershey's biggest dud has turned out to be new computer system", *The Wall Street Journal CIV*, vol. 85, pp. A1–A6, 1999.

[NGA 08] NAGAI E.W.T., LAW C.C.H., WAT F.K.T., "Examining the critical success factors in the adoption of enterprise resource planning", *Computers in Industry*, vol. 59, no. 6, pp. 548–564, 2008.

[O'CA 99] O'CALLAGHAN A.J., "Migrating large scale legacy systems to component-based and object technology: the evolution of a pattern language", *Communications of the AIS (Association for Information Systems)*, vol. 2, no. 3, pp. 1–43, 1999.

[OST 00] OSTERLAND A., "Blaming ERP", *CFO Magazine for Senior Financial Executives*, pp. 1–3, available at http://www.ismlab.usf.edu/isec/files/Risk-BlamingERP-CFO2000.pdf, January 2000.

[PAN 11] PANORAMA CONSULTING GROUP, ERP Report, available at http://panorama-consulting.com/Documents/2011-ERP-Report.pdf, 2011.

[PAP 03] PAPAZOGLOU M.P., GEORGAKOPOULOS D., "Service-oriented computing", *Communications ACM*, vol. 46, no. 10, pp. 25–28, October 2003.

[PAR 00] PARR A., SHANKS G., "A model of ERP project implementation", *Journal of Information Technology*, vol. 15, no. 4, pp. 289–304, 2000.

[PAR 05] PARK K., KUSIAK K., "Enterprise resource planning (ERP) operations support systems for maintaining process integration", *International Journal of Production Research*, vol. 43, no. 19, pp. 3959–3982, 2005.

[PAR 09] PARIJAT U., PRANAB K DAN., "ERP in Indian SME's: A Post Implementation Study of the Underlying Critical Success Factors", *International Journal Of Management Innovation System*, vol. 1, no. 2, pp. 1–10, 2009.

[PÉR 04] PÉROTIN P., Les progiciels de gestion intégrés, instrument de l'intégration organisationnelle?, Doctoral Thesis University of Montpellier II, available at http://hal.archives-ouvertes.fr/docs/00/04/79/40/PDF/tel-00008966.pdf, 2004.

[PIV 89] PIVNICNY V.C., CARMODY J.G., "Criteria help hospitals evaluate vendor proposals", *Healthcare Financial Management*, vol. 43, pp. 38–43, 1989.

[PLA 06] PLANT R., WILLCOCKS L., Critical success factors in international implementations: a case research approach, London School of Economics and Political Science, Working paper series no. 145, 2006.

[POS 88] POSTMAN N., *Conscientious Objections: Stirring up Trouble About Language, Technology and Education*, Alfred A. Knopf, New York, 1988.

[PRA 08] PRADELIER L., Comment l'organisation de l'entreprise influence-t-elle la structure du système d'information ? Jalons théoriques et méthodologiques, ESC Clermont notebook no. 1, 2008.

[PTA 00] PTAK C., SCHRAGENHEIM E., *ERP: Tools, Techniques, and Applications for Integrating the Supply Chain*, St. Lucie Press, Boca Raton, Fl, 2000.

[RAO 00] RAO S.S., "Enterprise resource planning: business needs and technologies", *Industrial Management and Data Systems*, vol. 100, nos. 1–2, pp. 81–88, 2000.

[RAS 05] RASMY M.H., THARWAT A., ASHRAF S., "Enterprise resource planning (ERP) implementation in the Egyptian organizational context", *European Mediterranean Conference on Information Systems*, Cairo, pp. 1–13, 2005.

[RAS 10] RASCHKE R.L., "Process-based view of agility: the value contribution of IT and the effects on process outcomes", *International Journal of Accounting Information Systems*, vol. 11, no. 4, pp. 297–313, available at http://dx.doi.org/10.1016/j.accinf.2010.09.005, 2010.

[RAT 12] RATKEVIČIUS D., RATKEVIČIUS Č., SKYRIUS R., "ERP selection criteria: theoretical and practical views", *Ekonomika*, vol. 91, no. 2, pp. 97–116, 2012.

[RET 07] RETTIG C., "The trouble with enterprise software", *MIT Sloan Management Review*, vol. 49, no. 1, pp. 21–27, 2007.

[ROB 11] ROBB D., Enterprise ERP buyer's guide: SAP, Oracle and Microsoft, available at: www.enterpriseappstoday.com, January 2011.

[ROB 13] ROBB D., Business intelligence buying guide for small businesses, available at http://www.enterpriscappstoday.com/business-intelligence/business-intelligence-buying-guide-smb-1.html, accessed 4 January 2013.

[ROD 98] RODIM VAN ES M., "Dynamic enterprise innovation – establishing continuous improvement in business", *Baan Business Innovation*, Modderkolk Ede Netherlands, 1998.

[ROG 94] ROGERSON S., FIDLER C., "Strategic information systems planning: its adoption and use", *Information Management & Computer Security Journal*, vol. 12, no. 3, pp. 12–17, 1994.

[ROS 00] ROSARIO J.G., "On the leading edge: critical success factors in ERP implementation projects", *Business World (Philippines)*, vol. 27, p. 27, 2000.

[ROS 01] ROSEMANN M., SEDERA W., GABLE G.G., "Critical Success Factors of Process Modeling for Enterprise Systems", *Americas Conference on Information Systems (AMCIS), Proceedings paper 218*, pp. 1128–1130, 2001.

[ROW 05] ROWE F., ELAMRANI R., BIDAN M. *et al.*, "Does ERP provide a cross-functional view of the firm? Challenging conventional wisdom for SMEs and large French firms", *26th International Conference on Information Systems*, Los Vegas, pp. 11–24, 2005.

[SAD 99] SADAGOPAN S., *The World of ERP: a Managerial Perspective*, Tata McGraw-Hill Publishing Company Limited, New Delhi, pp. 1–16, 1999.

[SAM 04] SAMARA T., Multiplicité des utilisateurs et pertinence des systèmes d'information multidimensionnels: l'exemple du secteur bancaire, Doctoral thesis, CNAM Paris, 2004.

[SCH 00] SCHONEFELD M., VERING O., "Enhancing ERP-efficiency through workflow-services", *Proceedings of 2000 Americas Conference on Information Systems*, AMCIS Long Island, CA, pp. 640–645, 2000.

[SCO 99] SCOTT E.J., "The FoxMeyer Drugs' bankruptcy: was it a failure of ERP?", *Proceedings of the 5th Americas Conference on Information System*, Milwaukee, WI, pp. 223–225, 13 May 1999.

[SHA 00] SHANG S., SEDDON P., "A comprehensive framework for classifying the benefits of ERP systems", *Americas Conference on Information Systems (AMCIS)*, vol. 39, pp. 2–10, 2000.

[SHA 05] SHARIF A.M., IRANI Z., LOVE P.E.D., "Integrating ERP using EAI: a model for post-hoc evaluation", *European Journal of Information Systems*, vol. 14, no. 3, pp. 162–174, 2005.

[SHA 09] SHAHIN D., SULAIMAN A., "Successful enterprise resource planning implementation: taxonomy of critical factors", *Industrial Management and Data Systems*, vol. 109, no. 8, pp. 1037–1052, 2009.

[SHE 04] SHEHAB E., SHARP M., SUPRAMANIAM L. *et al.*, "Enterprise resource planning: an integrative review", *Business Process Management Journal*, vol. 10, no. 4, pp. 359–386, 2004.

[SHO 05] SHOU Y., YING Y., "Critical failure factors of information system projects in Chinese enterprises", in CHEN J. (ed.), *International Conference on Services Systems and Services Management. Proceedings of ICSSSM'05*, IEEE Press, pp. 823–827, 2005.

[SIG 07] SIGGELKOW N., "Persuasion with case studies", *Academy of Management Journal*, vol. 50, pp. 20–24, 2007.

[SIR 00a] SIRIGINIDI S.R., "Enterprise resource planning: business needs and technologies", *Industrial Management & Data Systems*, vol. 100, p. 81, 2000.

[SIR 00b] SIRIGINIDI S.R., "Enterprise resource planning in reengineering business", *Business Process Management Journal*, vol. 6, p. 376, 2000.

[SOH 00] SOH C., KIEN S. S.,TAY-YAP J., "Enterprise resource planning: cultural fits and misfits: Is ERP a universal solution?", *Communications of the Association for Computing Machinery (ACM)*, vol. 43, no. 4, pp. 47–51, 1999.

[SOM 01] SOMERS T., NELSON K., "The impact of critical success factors across the stages of enterprise resource planning implementation", *Proceedings of the 34th Hawaii International Conference on System Sciences*, pp. 3775–3784, 2001.

[SPA 03] SPATHIS C., CONSTANTINIDES S., "The usefulness of ERP systems for effective management", *Industrial Management and Data Systems*, vol. 103, no. 9, pp. 677–685, 2003.

[SPA 04] SPATHIS C., CONSTANTINIDES S., "Enterprise resource planning systems' impact on accounting processes", *Business Process Management Journal*, vol. 10, no. 2, pp. 234–247, 2004.

[SPR 00] SPROTT D., "Componentizing the enterprise application packages", *Communication of the ACM*, vol. 43, no. 2, pp. 63–69, 2000.

[STA 04] STAPLETON G., REZAK C.J., "Change management underpins a successful ERP implementation at Marathon Oil", *Journal of Organization Excellence*, vol. 23, no. 4, pp. 15–21, 2004.

[STE 01] STENSRUD E., "Alternative approaches to effort prediction of ERP projects", *Information & Software Technology*, vol. 43, no. 7, pp. 413–423, 2001.

[SUM 00] SUMNER M., "Risk factors in enterprise-wide/ERP Projects", *Journal of Information Technology*, vol. 15, no. 4, pp. 317–327, 2000.

[SUM 99] SUMNER M., "Critical success factors in enterprise wide information management systems projects", *Proceedings of the Americas Conference on Information Systems*, Milwaukee, WI, pp. 232–234, 1999.

[SUN 05] SUN A.Y.T., YAZDANI A., OVEREND J.D., "Achievement assessment for enterprise resource planning (ERP) system implementations based on critical success factors (CSFs)", *International Journal of Production Economics*, vol. 98, no. 2, pp. 189–203, 2005.

[SWA 99] SWAN J., NEWELL S., ROBERTSON M., "The illusion of 'best practice' in information systems for operations management", *European Journal of Information Systems*, vol. 8, no. 8, pp. 284–293, December 1999.

[SWA 04] SWANTON B., "Build ERP upgrade costs into the business change program – not the IT budget", *Computer Weekly*, pp. 28–28, 21 September 2004.

[THE 00] THEMISTOCLEOUS M., IRANI Z., SHARIF A., "Evaluating application integration", *7th European Conference on Evaluation of Information Technology (ECITE 2000)*, pp. 193–202, 2000.

[THE 01] THEMISTOCLEOUS M., IRANI Z., O'KEEFE R.M., "ERP and application integration, exploratory survey", *Business Process Management Journal*, vol. 7, no. 3, pp. 195–204, 2001.

[THE 02] THEMISTOCLEOUS M., IRANI Z., LOVE P., "Enterprise application integration: an emerging technology for integrating ERP and supply chains", in WRYCZA S. (ed.), *Proceedings of the 10th European Conference on Information Systems (ECIS 2002), Information Systems and the Future of the Digital Economy*, Gdansk, Poland, pp. 1087–1096, 6–8 June 2002.

[TIW 06] TIWANA A., KEIL M., "Functionality risk in information systems development: an empirical investigation", *IEEE Transactions on Engineering Management*, vol. 53, no. 3, pp. 412–425, 2006.

[TRA 13] TRABELSI L., ABID HAMMAMI I., "Urbanization of information systems as a trigger for enhancing agility: a state in the Tunisian firms", *European Journal of Business and Management*, vol. 5, no. 5, pp. 63–77, 2013.

[TSA 05] TSAI W.H., CHIEN S.W., HSU P.Y. *et al.*, "Identification of critical failure factors in the implementation of enterprise resource planning (ERP) system in Taiwan's industries", *International Journal of Management and Enterprise Development*, vol. 2, no. 2, pp. 219–239, 2005.

[TSA 09a] TSAI W.H., SHEN Y.S., LEE P.L. *et al.*, "An empirical investigation of the impacts of ERP consultant selections and project management on ERP IS success assessment", *Proceedings of International Conference on Industrial Engineering and Engineering Management, IEEE*, Hong Kong, pp. 568–572, 2009.

[TSA 09b] TSAI W.H., LEE P.L., SHEN Y.S. *et al.*, "The relationship between ERP software selection criterion and ERP success", *Proceedings of International Conference on Industrial Engineering and Engineering Management, IEEE*, Hong Kong, pp. 2222–2226, 2009.

[TSA 09c] TSAI W.H., LIN S.J., LIN W.R. *et al.*, "The relationship between planning & control risk and ERP project success", *Proceedings of International Conference on Industrial Engineering and Engineering Management, IEEE*, Hong Kong, pp. 1835–1839, 2009.

[UFL 07] UFLACKER M., BUSSE D.K., "Complexity in enterprise applications vs. simplicity in user experience", *HCI 4*, vol. 4553, Lecture Notes in Computer Science, Springer, pp. 778–787, 2007.

[UMB 02] UMBLE E., UMBLE M., "Avoiding ERP implementation failure", *Industrial Management*, vol. 44, no. 1, pp. 25–33, 2002.

[UMB 03] UMBLE E.J., HAFT R.R., UMBLE M.M., "Enterprise resource planning: implementation procedures and critical success factors", *European Journal of Operational Research*, vol. 146, no. 2, pp. 241–257, 2003.

[VEN 10] VENTANA RESEARCH, Beware of performance management pitfalls smart companies avoids basic mistakes in implementation, available at http://www.ventanaresearch.com/assets/0/71/112/113/6299275f-0215-4380-adc99f641e21603f.pdf, 2010.

[VER 02] VERVILLE J., HALINGTEN A., "An investigation of the decision process for selecting an ERP software: the case of ESC", *Management Decision*, vol. 40, no. 3, pp. 206–216, 2002.

[VER 03] VERVILLE J., HALINGTEN A., "A six-stage model of the buying process for ERP software", *Industrial Marketing Management*, vol. 32, no. 7, pp. 585–594, 2003.

[WAI 09] WAILGUM T., 10 famous ERP disasters, dustups and disappointments, CIO, available at http://www.cio.com, 24 March 2009.

[WAN 07] WANG E.T.G., LIN C.C.L., JIANGB J.J. *et al.*, "Improving enterprise resource planning (ERP) fit to organizational process through knowledge transfer", *International Journal of Information Management*, vol. 27, no. 3, pp. 200–212, 2007.

[WEI 02] WEISS T.R., SONGINI M.L., "Hershey upgrades R/3 ERP system without hitches", *Computerworld*, vol. 36, no. 37, 9 September 2002.

[WEI 04] WEI C.C., WANG M.J.J., "A comprehensive framework for selecting an ERP system", *International Journal of Project Management*, vol. 22, pp. 161–169, 2004.

[WEI 05] WEI C.C., CHIEN C.F., WANG M.J.J., "An AHP-based approach to ERP system selection", *International Journal of Production Economics*, vol. 96, no. 1, pp. 47–62, 2005.

[WEI 08] WEILING K., KWOK KEE W., "Organizational culture and leadership in ERP implementation", *Decision Support Systems*, vol. 45, no. 2, pp. 208–218, 2008.

[WIE 07] WIER B., HUNTON J., HASSABELNABY H.R., "Enterprise resource planning systems and non-financial performance incentives: the joint impact on corporate performance", *International Journal of Accounting Information Systems*, vol. 8, no. 3, pp. 165–190, 2007.

[WIL 00] WILLCOCKS L.P., SYKES R., "The role of the CIO and IT function in ERP", *Communications of the ACM*, vol. 43, no. 4, pp. 32–38, 2000.

[WON 03] WONG B., TEIN D., "Critical success factors for ERP projects", *Proceedings of the National Conference of the Australian Institute of Project Management*, pp. 1–8, available at http://cms.3rdgen.info/3rdgen_sites/107/resource/orwongandtein.pdf, 2003.

[WOO 07] WOO H., "Critical success factors for implementing ERP: the case of a Chinese electronics' manufacturer", *Journal of Manufacturing Technology Management*, vol. 18, no. 4, pp. 431–442, 2007.

[WOR 07] WORLD ECONOMIC FORUM, The global information technology report 2006–2007, available at http://www.greaterzuricharea.ch/content/05/downloads/2007_nri_wef.pdf, 2007.

[YAJ 05] YAJIONG X., HUIGANG L., WILLIAM R. *et al.*, "ERP implementation failures in China: case studies with implications for ERP vendors", *International Journal of Production Economics*, vol. 97, no. 3, pp. 279–295, 2005.

[YAN 07] YANG J.B., WU C.T., TSAI C.H., "Selection of an ERP system for a construction firm in Taiwan: a case study", *Automation in Construction*, vol. 16, no. 6, pp. 787–796, 2007.

[YEO 02] YEO K., "Critical failure factors in information system projects", *International Journal of Project Management*, vol. 20, no. 3, pp. 241–246, 2002.

[YIN 04] YIN R.K., "Case study methods", in GREEN J.L., CAMILLI G., ELMORE P.B. (eds), *Complementary Methods for Research in Education*, Lawrence Erlbaum Association, 3rd ed., 2004.

[ZET 04] ZETIE C., BARNETT L., Why enterprise application development is so hard – and how it must get easier, Internal report, Forrester Research Inc., August 2004.

[ZHA 02] ZHANG L., LEE K.O., BANERJEE P., "Critical success factors of enterprise resource planning systems implementation success in China", *Proceedings of the 36th Hawaii International Conference on System Sciences*, pp. 1–10, 2002.

[ZIA 06] ZIAEE M., FATHIAN M., SADJADI S.J., "A modular approach to ERP system selection: a case study", *Information Management & Computer Security*, vol. 14, no. 5, pp. 485–495, 2006.

Index

Other titles from

in

Information Systems, Web and Pervasive Computing

2015

ARDUIN Pierre-Emmanuel, GRUNDSTEIN Michel,
ROSENTHAL-SABROUX Camille
Information and Knowledge System

BÉRANGER Jérôme
Medical Information Systems Ethics

IAFRATE Fernando
From Big Data to Smart Data

POMEROL Jean-Charles, EPELBOIN Yves, THOURY Claire
MOOCs

SALLES Maryse
Decision-Making and the Information System

2014

DINET Jérôme
Information Retrieval in Digital Environments

HÉNO Raphaële, CHANDELIER Laure
3D Modeling of Buildings: Outstanding Sites

KEMBELLEC Gérald, CHARTRON Ghislaine, SALEH Imad
Recommender Systems

MATHIAN Hélène, SANDERS Lena
Spatio-temporal Approaches: Geographic Objects and Change Process

PLANTIN Jean-Christophe
Participatory Mapping

VENTRE Daniel
Chinese Cybersecurity and Defense

2013

BERNIK Igor
Cybercrime and Cyberwarfare

CAPET Philippe, DELAVALLADE Thomas
Information Evaluation

LEBRATY Jean-Fabrice, LOBRE-LEBRATY Katia
Crowdsourcing: One Step Beyond

SALLABERRY Christian
Geographical Information Retrieval in Textual Corpora

2012

BUCHER Bénédicte, LE BER Florence
Innovative Software Development in GIS

GAUSSIER Eric, YVON François
Textual Information Access

STOCKINGER Peter
Audiovisual Archives: Digital Text and Discourse Analysis

VENTRE Daniel
Cyber Conflict

2011

BANOS Arnaud, THÉVENIN Thomas
Geographical Information and Urban Transport Systems

DAUPHINÉ André
Fractal Geography

LEMBERGER Pirmin, MOREL Mederic
Managing Complexity of Information Systems

STOCKINGER Peter
Introduction to Audiovisual Archives

STOCKINGER Peter
Digital Audiovisual Archives

VENTRE Daniel
Cyberwar and Information Warfare

2010

BONNET Pierre
Enterprise Data Governance

BRUNET Roger
Sustainable Geography

CARREGA Pierre
Geographical Information and Climatology

CAUVIN Colette, ESCOBAR Francisco, SERRADJ Aziz
Thematic Cartography – 3-volume series
Thematic Cartography and Transformations – volume 1
Cartography and the Impact of the Quantitative Revolution – volume 2
New Approaches in Thematic Cartography – volume 3

LANGLOIS Patrice
Simulation of Complex Systems in GIS

MATHIS Philippe
Graphs and Networks – 2nd edition

THÉRIAULT Marius, DES ROSIERS François
Modeling Urban Dynamics

2009

BONNET Pierre, DETAVERNIER Jean-Michel, VAUQUIER Dominique
Sustainable IT Architecture: the Progressive Way of Overhauling Information Systems with SOA

PAPY Fabrice
Information Science

RIVARD François, ABOU HARB Georges, MERET Philippe
The Transverse Information System

ROCHE Stéphane, CARON Claude
Organizational Facets of GIS

VENTRE Daniel
Information Warfare

2008

BRUGNOT Gérard
Spatial Management of Risks

FINKE Gerd
Operations Research and Networks

GUERMOND Yves
Modeling Process in Geography

KANEVSKI Michael
Advanced Mapping of Environmental Data

MANOUVRIER Bernard, LAURENT Ménard
Application Integration: EAI, B2B, BPM and SOA

PAPY Fabrice
Digital Libraries

2007

DOBESCH Hartwig, DUMOLARD Pierre, DYRAS Izabela
Spatial Interpolation for Climate Data

SANDERS Lena
Models in Spatial Analysis

2006

CLIQUET Gérard
Geomarketing

CORNIOU Jean-Pierre
Looking Back and Going Forward in IT

DEVILLERS Rodolphe, JEANSOULIN Robert
Fundamentals of Spatial Data Quality

Printed and bound by CPI Group (UK) Ltd, Croydon, CR0 4YY

27/10/2024

14580729-0002